Praise for *Life after Art*

Life after Art will help you recover what was lost or stolen from your childhood throughout the arduous journey of life. Reclaim the untainted creativity, imagination, and optimism of your youth—and discover the very person you were meant to be.

—BEN ARMENT
Creator of *STORY* conference and *Dream Year*

How many years has it been since you were covered in paint in your elementary school's art room? After reading *Life after Art,* you may want to go back. Matt takes readers on a journey to the art room to discover our purpose in life which can be found in our God-given ability to create beauty for the world to see.

—ANNE JACKSON
Speaker and author of *Permission to Speak Freely: Essays & Art on Fear, Confession & Grace,* and *Mad Church Disease: Overcoming the Burnout Epidemic*

As someone who is trying to be an artist, this book spoke to me. As a dad of two creative daughters, this spoke to me. As a Christian, this spoke to me. The bottom line is that Matt's written a book that communicates an important hope. And it will speak to you too.

—JON ACUFF
Speaker and *Wall Str*
Quitter and *Stuff Chr*

Matt has written the book   ken
art and made it grace. He's   ...an-
ity. He's taken adults and made them children, again. With

thoughtful questions, humorous anecdotes, and crisp story telling, Matt paints a picture of what heaven can look like on earth. In the same way I frame my paintings, I wish I could frame the message of *Life after Art* and hang it on my walls for all the world to see. This book has been a long time coming and it will make artists out of all of us.

> **—EMILY WIERENGA**
> Award-winning journalist, artist, and author of *Save My Children* and *Chasing Silhouettes*

Our time-obsessed culture of productivity has piled so much upon our adult lives that we've let slip the things that truly enhance our spiritual, emotional, and even physical well-being. Matt Appling's call to return to the timeless joy of making beautiful things is powerful. More art. More creating. More mess. As a visual artist and a grown-up overcome with responsibilities, this is a message I needed to hear.

> **—JASON BOYETT**
> Author of *O Me of Little Faith* and *Pocket Guide to the Afterlife*

What I love about this book is its commitment to call out the best in each of us. All of us want to live the extraordinary life Jesus promises, but many miss out on it because of hurt, failure or disappointment. *Life after Art* commissions us to recapture God's vision for our life and pursue it with passion.

> **—JUSTIN DAVIS**
> Cofounder of RefineUs Ministries and coauthor of *Beyond Ordinary: When a Good Marriage Just Isn't Good Enough*

When we were kids we were told we were artists, but over time we forgot how to be artists. Matt reminds us that being an artist and making a life filled with beauty should no longer be relegated to our kindergarten classes. In my humble opinion, being an artist means changing the world, and Matt's book will help you do exactly that.

—**Blaine Hogan**
> Creative director, actor, artist and author of *UNTITLED: Thoughts on the Creative Process*

Relearn what you have been taught to forget. Allow the art of your life to greater speak so others can see what they cannot hear. Journey with Matt and explore life and faith through one of the most powerful mediums on the face of the earth today, the arts.

—**Eric Samuel Timm**
> Communicator, artist, founder of No One Underground and Painting Hope

Matt Appling's voice is charismatic, enthusiastic, and refreshingly honest. He addresses a host of issues including creativity, postmodernism, failure, and beauty with earnestness, simplicity, and a keen sense of humor. However, what is truly unique about this book is the Christian worldview he applies through story to inspire you as a creator.

—**G. James Daichendt, EdD**
> Professor at Azusa Pacific University and author of *Artist-Teacher: A Philosophy for Creating and Teaching*

I wish I could go back to kindergarten and be in Mr. Appling's art class. But reading Matt's book, I kind of can. *Life after Art* is a simple and compelling message, reminding my grown-up self that I have everything I need to create beauty in the world with my work, my faith, and my life—an insightful and encouraging read.

—**EMILY P. FREEMAN**

Speaker and author of *Grace for the Good Girl: Letting Go of the Try-Hard Life*

This book is a tremendous resource for any creative who can identify with having vibrant dreams as a child, but you've lost it and feel creatively stuck as an adult. *Life after Art* will reveal some powerful truths towards helping you find fulfillment and discover the life you were created for.

—**PETE WILSON**

Founding pastor of Cross Point Church, communicator, and author of *Plan B* and *Empty Promises*

LIFE after *ART*

what you forgot about life and faith
since you left the art room

MATT APPLING

MOODY PUBLISHERS
CHICAGO

Edited by Brandon O'Brien
Cover design: Connie Gabbert Design and Illustration
Cover image: Connie Gabbert
Interior design: Smartt Guys design

ISBN: 978-0-8024-0739-9

We hope you enjoy this book from Moody Publishers. Our goal is to provide high-
quality, thought-provoking books and products that connect truth to your real needs
and challenges. For more information on other books and products written and
produced from a biblical perspective, go to www.moodypublishers.com or write to:

Moody Publishers
820 N. LaSalle Boulevard
Chicago, IL 60610

Moody Publishers is committed to caring wisely for God's creation
and uses recycled paper whenever possible. The paper in this book
consists of 10 percent post-consumer waste.

1 3 5 7 9 10 8 6 4 2

Printed in the United States of America

For all the beauty-makers in the world,
most especially the people who have made my world beautiful:
my parents and brother who drew the earliest designs on my life,
and my wife, Cheri,
who adds vibrant, joyful, beautiful color to my every day.

CONTENTS

Chapter Four: Coloring inside the Lines

Relearning how to create within the boundaries of life

Chapter Five: Freedom to Fail

Relearning how to take necessary risks

Chapter Six: Born to Create

Relearning how to be a creator

INTRODUCTION

It's four o' clock in the afternoon and my office is a mess. Scraps of paper litter the floor, as if a windstorm has blown through the room. The walls are smudged with fingerprints. My own hands are stained and my fingernails are caked with paint and chalk and ink. I wear an apron with dozens of colorful scars. I hang the apron on its hook, flip the light switch, and lock the door with a sense of satisfaction. The mess around the room is evidence of the day's accomplishments.

That's because my workplace is not a tidy cubicle with a little plant on my desk.

I am an art teacher.

It is no small task to lead children in creative pursuits, to give them tools and skills they can use one day to express their own ideas. Teaching art can be at the same time challenging, rewarding, frustrating, satisfying, even holy and worshipful. It's serious stuff! This is not arts and crafts at Vacation Bible School, kids. This room is a glitter-free zone, no exceptions.

I give a lot of high fives for jobs well done. I like to hold up a student's hard work and loudly declare his praises in front of the class. But I also have high standards for students because I feel a sense of ownership over the kids' work. It reflects on me as a teacher when I hang it up for all to see.

I have one overarching rule that I practice in my art class:

Art is for everyone.

I tell that to every parent who visits me. I tell that to the students. My room is not just for artsy and creative kids. It is for everyone to enjoy. No one gets left out.

Likewise, you can be sure that even if you are not particularly artsy or creative, even if you have not picked up a paintbrush or crayon since you last set foot in an art room, this *book* is for you too. If you are a businessman or a homemaker or a truck driver or a writer or a teacher or a restaurant server, this book is for you. No one gets left out here either.

See, the secret of my art room is that I don't really teach art. I am not training a bunch of future artists. I know most of my students will become teachers, doctors, lawyers, bankers, parents, and a million other things.

I am not training them for a lifetime of art.

I am training them for *life after art.*

A student's life after art begins on the last day of sixth grade. From their first day of kindergarten, I am looking ahead to that day when they walk out the door, never to return to the art room again. What do I want students to remember as they grow into young adults?

You and I are already living life after art. Odds are that at one time, like me, you were an elementary school student. And perhaps once a week we all sat in the school's art room. We drew pictures. We painted. We created. Maybe you have fond memories of those days. Maybe you hardly remember them at all.

You probably have not done any of those art room activities in a long time. Chances are good that it has been years, even decades, since you last left your school's art room. It has been years for me too.

What do I want my students to remember as they enter life after art?

I want them to remember all the things that I forgot.

There are a lot of things you and I used to know about life and faith and the world. No one taught us these things, they were just given to us by our Creator. But over the years, this native knowledge about the world around us got covered up. And that has shaped and colored our lives in negative ways ever since then.

All is not lost, though.

It turns out that the art room, which we left so long ago and probably have not thought much of since, is the exact place we need to return to. We need to return to the art room to rediscover what we have been missing. This book is not about arts and crafts or "creativity" in the sense you are probably thinking of it. This is a book about faith, family, hope, disappointment, dreams, failures, and all the other things that make up adult life.

So as you read along with me, I encourage you to place yourself in the art room again. Think about yourself sitting in your own school's art room all those years ago. Really exercise your memory and go back to first or second grade or even kindergarten with me, if your memory will stretch that far. Don't worry, it'll be fun, and you probably won't wet your pants like you did that one time. . . .

You might not think the art room has much to say to adults. What lessons could possibly be learned? The fact is: I had to grow up, leave home, get married, start a career, buy a house, pay bills, and forget about art for years *before* becoming an art teacher and discovering what I had been missing the whole time—the profound truths that the art room has to teach all of us who are living *life after art.*

CHAPTER ONE

All Children
Are *ARTISTS*

why we are all born naturally creative

1.1 Born to Be Something

Some people are born athletes. It is just in their DNA, a card in the hand they were dealt at birth. Others are born to be doctors and inventors or farmers and builders.

It seems that I was born to be an artist.

I was a pretty inventive child. When I was a little kid, sitting on the living room rug, I loved to build things with blocks. When I was older and had a lot more blocks and playthings, my creations and buildings would cover the living room.

And while I did well in school, the art room really became my home. I have sat in many art rooms over the years. Some left something to be desired. My first art room, in a poor rural school, was limited to just one piece of paper per child per day.

One day, we arrived to art class to find that only green paint was available to us that day.

Some art rooms were really wonderful places. I had a phenomenal art teacher at the school we moved to in the city. I do not remember more than a few bits and pieces of art lessons, but I remember how that art room *felt*.

Do you remember how your favorite teacher made you *feel*? I remember how it felt to be my art teacher's student. She had a wonderful, warm personality. She made me feel like I was her favorite student.

I think she made all of us feel that way.

Her art room was a sanctuary that reflected her caring spirit, with lots of personal touches. The one detail I remember most was that she had placed the word "EMPATHY" in rather small letters on the ceiling. She never mentioned why it was there, and I am guessing most children did not even notice it. But I did.

Despite the art room being my natural home, art class is, of course, only an hour a week. And art never won a kid any popularity contests. It was strange how the same kids who were shocked and amazed by my artwork could jeer and harass me in P.E. I just wasn't dealt a very even hand of cards. You could not find a less athletic child than me. It made no sense that the same hands that naturally could paint and draw could not throw a ball accurately to save my life. As I began to fully grasp my athletic shortcomings, the gym would become my own little slice of elementary school hell. The art room was my refuge.

1.2 **All Children Are Born Artists**

What kind of a kid were you?

Perhaps, unlike me, you were the kind of child who did *not* take refuge in the art room. Maybe your school days revolved around your next chance to go to P.E. or recess, to throw things and run around. You may have been the kind of kid who liked to play in the mud and climb trees. Or maybe you played with dolls or action figures. Were you a solitary child, or were you a child who had a secret club with the kids next door? Kids come in all shapes and sizes and variety. But all children have some things in common that make them *kids*.

When I became an art teacher, one of my first jobs was to decorate my classroom. I wanted my room to show everyone how highly I felt about art and my students. So on the wall of my art classroom, I painted in large purple letters a partial quote from the renowned painter Pablo Picasso:

"All children are born artists . . ."

Do you believe that? Maybe you never thought of yourself as an artist. Can Picasso really paint all children with such a broad brush? I think Picasso must have been right. Because no matter what kinds of kids you and I were, whatever we enjoyed doing, chances are we were at our best when we were *creating* something.

Children are natural creators. In fact, all of us were creating before we even knew what the word meant. Children make up stories and games. They create characters, heroes and villains, and fabulous made-up places to live in. While some kids build with blocks, others play "house" or host tea parties. A child's world is a surreal place where imagination swirls and blurs with reality.

The only difference between most kids is *what* they like to create.

I was building with blocks and drawing pictures. What were you creating when you were five years old? Were you creating stories or playing house or making up games or covering the fridge with paintings?

Yes, Picasso must have been right. This drive to create things, to re-create the world as we see fit, to play pretend—it must be in our genetic code. Simply put a few crayons or some paint in front of a child and she will know what to do with them. When most children come to kindergarten, they have creative energy to spare, and with a little leading, all children can create.

Children even surprise me with their creations. They do it regularly. They see things differently. They exceed my expectations. They make something unexpected.

For that matter, teachers and parents could take away every "creative" item in a room, and children will still create surprising things. Sticks, rocks, or even random debris on the playground are constantly transformed into dolls, magical items, weapons, or any number of things adults would never think of.

Through adult eyes, these activities may appear to be silly child's play, but I want you to think of even these childish activities as "creating."

That is not such a leap, is it? When adults go to a movie, what are we watching? We are watching other adults act like children, essentially. A writer and director made up a story. The actors are pretending that they are in danger or in love. The costume artists are playing dress up. The prop artists are making weapons and magical items out of metal, rubber, foam, and even random debris. The set designers are creating a whole world from their imaginations. When you and I go to the movies, we are paying good money (earned in the *real* world) to watch adults, in essence, act like children. To put it another way, we're watching adults who have become *very practiced* at doing the same things that five-year-olds do.

1.3 Born to Take Risks

Children are not just naturally creative, but many of them are also natural risk takers. How many near heart attacks did you give your mother by climbing onto some too-high place? As a teenager, how many risks—that you would now call "stupid"— did you take? Though we want children to be careful and safe, risk-taking is a critical part of child development. Even the most cautious child must be taught to take a risk, to jump off the high dive at the swimming pool, or speak to the new kid at school, to try difficult things.

I was an exceptionally cautious and deliberate child, but risk-taking was still a part of my development. I slowly learned that if I ever wanted something, a measure of risk was sure to be required. As a thirteen-year-old, I learned I would have to risk getting punched if I wanted to stand up to a bully (which I did). As a teenager, I would have to risk my pride if I wanted a date with a girl. As an adult, I would have to risk rejection if I wanted a job. And as a child, if I didn't want to get struck by lightning, I would have to jump off the diving board.

Yes, one of the risk-taking lessons most vividly imprinted on my mind involves the diving board and an impending lightning storm.

My brother and I were at the apartment complex's pool with my mother, having a great time. I had been thinking about jumping off the diving board all afternoon, but as a skinny, craven seven-year-old, I had not done so yet. Finally my mother decided she had enough of seeing me approach the diving board and backing away. She told me that I would have to jump before we left.

As I stood, shivering on the board, lips turning blue, I continued to think and hesitate, and my mother grew impatient. She began goading me every time I tried to back away from the edge. And there was an angry looking storm quickly approaching. She told me the requirement stood: I would have to jump off the board before we went inside. Lightning started to flash and the rain began to come down and she told me I was likely to be struck, standing up on that board.

If I got struck by lightning, I would be in big trouble with Mom.

So, thanks to the fear of an imminent lightning strike, I quickly jumped, scurried out of the pool, and we all scrambled inside.

Some kids may be cowards like I was. Some kids may be painfully shy. But of all the risks a child can take, creating might be the riskiest. And that is a risk that children always seem to be willing to take.

Think about how risky *creating* something is. It is much riskier than your chances of being struck by lightning. When you create a story or a song or a painting or a gift, you are opening up your mind, heart, and soul to the scrutiny of others. Perhaps your audience will love your creation. But you are inviting criticism or rejection. This fact almost never seems to occur to children though. Even the shyest or most cowardly children are naturally *generous* with their creations. Anything a child creates becomes something to *give* to someone they love.

What good is it to make up a game without someone to play it? What sense is there for a child to create a puppet without an audience to watch a puppet show? Why would a little girl meticulously set a table if she were not planning on inviting Daddy to her room for tea? What child paints a picture and then refuses to let Mom hang it on the fridge?

From watching students in my classroom, it is abundantly clear to me that they simply cannot wait to show off everything they create. They want to show off their work to me. They want to show off to their friends. They want to show off to their parents. You and I were probably the same way when we were their age. When we were children, we probably could not wait to show off everything we created. If we made a card for Mother's Day or a Christmas gift for Dad, we were proud of our work. Kindergartners are practically *too* eager to show off their work, even when it's still in progress. They are so excited to bring their projects home, they are almost disappointed when paint has to dry, or I insist on hanging their work in the hallway for a week. They are eager to share their art with the people who are most important to them.

They are desperate to be generous, to share what they have created.

1.4 Completely Unaware

Why are children so generous and eager to share their creativity? Probably because they lack a whole lot of self-consciousness.

When five-year-olds go to P.E. or recess to create and play games, they never seem to be thinking about whether they are *good* or *bad* at playing games. It does not seem to occur to them that they might look silly while playing. They just play because it is fun to do so.

Likewise, when five-year-olds go to music class, they sing, not because they know that they are *good* or *bad* singers, because most five-year-olds sound sort of alike—that is to say, *bad*. It appears that they sing because they just *enjoy* the act of singing.

And in art class, five-year-olds never seem to be thinking about how *good* or *bad* they are. They rarely compare their art to anyone else's. I almost never hear a kindergartner say he's unhappy with his work. I ask children at the end of the hour what they are *proud of* about their work, and twenty little hands shoot up, eager to show off.

Children really just are not aware if they are *good* or *bad* at anything!

That's probably just as well. Interpreting children's artwork usually requires a bit of extra imagination on the part of the adults around them. Kindergartners have handed me self-portraits that looked like they were demon-possessed. And while they could not be prouder and their smiles could not be bigger, I wondered if I could hang their nightmare-inducing projects on the wall.

It is this naïveté that allows children to create freely and joyfully, and so eagerly share their art with abandon.

To summarize: as five-year-olds, most of us had uncanny creative drives, we were generous with what we created, and we created with abandon and lack of self-awareness.

Think about the five-year-old version of yourself for one more minute. There is a lot of time and distance between five-year-old you and yourself today. This is the "you" before high school, before awkward teen romance and unrequited love, when boys and girls still had "cooties." This was before you settled on a career. This was before you worried about bills or insurance or mortgages. You only had childhood worries and concerns. You were a creative child of some kind. I promise, you were. What were you creating? And you were generous with your creations. You couldn't wait to show off what you had made to the people you cared about. Who were you most eager to share with? And you had no awareness if anything you made was good or bad.

Creating just made you incredibly, unabashedly *happy, fulfilled, and satisfied.*

Think about five-year-old you running around the playground, or singing your lungs out in music class, or smearing paint on paper in the art room. It was all so joyful and carefree. A lot has happened since then. Five-year-old you has been covered up under layers of dust accumulated over many years.

That moment in time so long ago was the freest you have ever been in your entire life.

This book is about rediscovering and living in that moment.

QUESTIONS FOR THOUGHT

1. What did you enjoy creating as a child?

2. With whom did you share your creations?

CHAPTER TWO

The Challenge Is to *STAY* an *ARTIST* as an *ADULT*

how we lose our naturally born creativity

2.1 Art Belongs to Me

Since I had few talents outside of art, I began to take real owner-ship of it as I discovered the extent of my abilities. I began to feel that art was "mine."

My little brother, on the other hand, much like the rest of the family, had not one artistic bone in his body. But, as little broth-ers are prone to do, he wanted to emulate his big brother. Mom and Dad bought him some art supplies, a humble little drawing pad and some pencils.

This outlandish act of parental nurturing was met with a lot of protestations and righteous indignation from me. I showed Mom and Dad that they were wasting their money, better spent on supplies for *me.* I deftly pointed out that he was athletic and should stick to *his* activities. Furthermore, as I demonstrated with "exhibit A," his drawings of "people" were barely recognizable lumps and squiggles. Conclusion: his innate lack of talent did not entitle him to "my" activity.

Case closed.

By Aaron
First Grade

EXHIBIT A: *A Halloween Scene, by my brother, Aaron, age six. Note the crude implementation of line and shape, the lack of attention to anatomical correctness, and the general sense that nurturing this child's artistic pursuits would be a complete waste of time, in my opinion.*

But my airtight case fell on my parents' deaf ears, and my brother was encouraged to continue (futilely) exploring art. "Mistrial!" I cried.

However, my brother gave up on art after a few weeks, maybe less. I scooped up his nearly new art pencils from under his bed and added them to my collection, satisfied that I had put my brother in his place.

Sometime later, my brother began to become a better, smarter student than he had been before. He had always been scatter-brained and unreliable in school, but he suddenly began to get better at completing his homework, much to the relief of my parents. However, I again insisted that being smart and a good student was *my* domain, and he was better suited to be the stupid child of the family.

Again, my logic was lost on everyone, and my brother turned out to be quite intelligent and studious and reasonably successful in life, which I no longer protest.

The irony of my early attitude about art is not lost on me. (As if my brother having a sketch pad somehow took art away from me.) It was the same childish pride that led me to think I was somehow more special in church because Dad was the one speaking from the pulpit.

Now, I am an ambassador of art, an evangelist of art. The student who resembles my brother is squarely in my crosshairs. My goal is no longer to force him out of the art room but to keep him *in* the art room as long as possible.

2.2 The Challenge Is to Stay an Artist as an Adult

In the last chapter, I asked you to remember the five-year-old version of yourself; the "you" who was, at one time, unabashedly, joyfully, generously creative.

Of course kindergartners become first graders, and first graders become second graders and so on. Despite all the doubts their parents face, children eventually grow up. Each day, you grow further from your kindergarten self.

Along the way, children gain a lot of knowledge, skills, and confidence. But there is a lot that is covered up, forgotten and lost along the way too.

This phenomenon of losing things as we grow up is a lot like swimming lessons.

Every summer, thousands of children go to their local pools to learn to kick and float and blow bubbles. It is an annual summer tradition. But why do children have to take swimming lessons? It may sound like nonsense, but these children are all learning skills that they used to have, and then forgot.

When babies are born, they have only a few reflexes, each designed for survival. When it comes to water, a baby will instinctively hold its breath for a short time when submerged. A baby placed stomach-side down in the water will respond with repetitive kicking and paddling. Babies do not have to be taught these things. **Please don't submerge your baby in the bathtub to try this.**

The interesting thing is these two instinctual behaviors disappear at about six months of age. They are lost and must be relearned at the city pool. Hundreds of children, holding their noses underwater, wiping water from their eyes, collectively pee-ing in giant chlorinated bathtubs, used to have no problem in the water.

Being able to swim is just one of the many things that we lose as we grow.

Or think of this:

One day Jesus was out on the town, teaching and talking with lots of people. When some children ran up to see Him, the adults were horrified, because this was a time when children were to be *seen* and not *heard*. So they tried to shoo the kiddos away before they got their dirty paws all over Jesus' new cloak (my summary). And what did Jesus do?

He commended the children.

He told the adults they need to become more like *the children*.

Jesus didn't get too specific about what He meant by that, but it was a shocking statement. Children were among the least regarded members of that society. If you wanted to be a great per-son, you did *not* emulate the humble social standing of a child.

But when Jesus looked into the eyes of the children, He saw something in them the adults lacked. Whatever the children had, it was nothing that had ever been *taught* to them. Who would teach them, the adults? Their Sunday school teachers? No, Jesus saw something *intrinsic* to the spirit of children.

By contrast, when Jesus looked at the adults, He saw a bunch of *former* five-year-olds. If they ever had that childlike spirit, it had been covered up with years and beards and dust and grime. Jesus went around telling adults that they must *become like children*, as if they must do more than gain something, but *regain* something that has been lost and forgotten amidst their years and learning and experiences of life.

2.3 The Great Disappearing Artist Trick

"I don't understand. He used to love art."

I was an inexperienced art teacher suffering from a lack of confidence the first time a mother told me, more or less, that I had crushed her son's love of art. He used to beam with pride over his bold works of art. Now he was apathetic, making lazy scribbles that his mother retrieved from the garbage can at home. She was even thinking of transferring him to a different school. Because of me! Because *I* had failed as an art teacher!

I took it hard. I thought I must be a terrible teacher. How could I accomplish the *exact opposite* of my mission? How could I extinguish the flame of creativity in this student?

That was not the last time parents called me or scheduled conferences with me to discuss their child's newfound indifference in art class. Every time, it broke my confidence a little more. I agonized and wondered where I was going wrong. Like a modern day Old Testament prophet, I went home and put on sweatpants and ashes and mourned the fate of my students.

That is, until I talked to the music teacher.

"Oh, I hear that one too. 'My child used to love music,'" she whispered, with a hint of irony. Now that surprised me, because I cannot imagine that this teacher is mean or cruel or sets out to destroy a child's love of music.

And then I noticed the kids in gym class. Some played

enthusiastically, while others looked as if they were being tortured. They hung out on the sidelines, waiting anxiously to be released back to class. They reminded me of myself at that age.

I started to see a pattern.

"Tell me what you are proud of about your art today."

I asked the kindergartners the same question yesterday, but there are far fewer hands raised today. That's because these are *former* kindergartners. They are sixth graders, mere shells of their five-year-old selves. Their childishness is being slowly covered by years and patchy facial hair and body odor.

It is almost exclusively from this age group, the fifth and sixth graders, that I will receive phone calls from parents about their child's dwindling interest in art. I never get calls from kindergarten parents.

The preteens, unlike kindergartners, provide only a few proud answers to my question. I hear a lot of vague answers to the effect of, "I don't like my project." Nothing specific, just a general sense of unease and dissatisfaction.

It's the same in music class and P.E. These artists and musicians and athletes are simply growing up. And they are losing their touch along the way. When a student no longer loves art, it has very little to do with me as a teacher, and there is also little I can do to stop the loss of interest.

Remember those three childhood traits discussed in chapter 1? Here they are again in case you forgot:

Creating was important to you.

You were generous with your creations.

You lacked self-consciousness in your creating.

Those three traits are what make every child an artist, and it is losing those traits that makes the artist in all of us disappear. It's much the same as why children must take swimming lessons, or why Jesus told the adults they needed to become like children again. This chapter is about how you lost and forgot those traits along your journey to adulthood. You have been missing them for a long time, and you have been suffering for it your entire adult life.

2.4 Creating Is Not Important

Today I am faced with a large group of prospective kindergarten parents. They are getting a tour of the school, and every tour group makes a stop at my room. They ask questions about the art program. I give my little rehearsed speech about how important I believe art is and give them a sense of what we do in my room.

Of course *I* think art is important. The problem is that to every other adult in the school, art is not as important as it is to me. Try being an art teacher and attempting to sound important to a lawyer or a doctor. Inside, I feel like a glorified babysitter. Creating often feels out of place in the world of adults, a curious relic of our innocent pasts. Creating seems like *child's play*.

That's the first thing that happens on our way to adulthood: creating things stops being a priority.

Bit by bit, little by little, you and I lost our childish creative drives. Other things became more important, and creating becomes *less*. We may have started by investing more in goofing off with friends. Then those hormones kicked in and threw our worlds and priorities into a tailspin. Before long, extending our educational or career pursuits became the number one priority. Then bills and mortgages and debts took over. And here we now sit as adults, you and I, with a million little priorities and concerns bearing on our minds. Your mind is filled with short-term tasks that gnaw away at your days and long-term goals that you worry you will never reach, and creating things like you did in your childhood is likely far from your mind. For most adults, creating has been long relegated to the world of child's play.

Maybe it should be no surprise that when schools and districts fall into financial trouble, it is often the art program that is the first to have its head on the chopping block. The art room is surrounded by the adult world, and its fate is decided by adults for whom creating has long lost its importance. Efficiency and bottom lines and state standards are the operating systems of adult life.

I wonder how many art teachers have resigned themselves to this sad conclusion—that what they teach is not really important, not *necessary*, just icing on the cake. They spend their days in underappreciated rooms filled with students taking a "less-important" class. And when funding runs dry, they're the first ones out of a job.

2.5 Art Is Not Creative

I can start these kindergartners off on the right foot by dashing their parents' opinions of art on day one.

"Art is so wonderful! It is just a great time to be creative," some mother gushes to me. She means well, but I feel the unmistakable need to set this mother straight.

"Well . . ." I struggle to be tactful. "We also learn quite a bit about how to use elements of art and design."

"Oh certainly!" she replies. "The art room is so much freer than regular schoolwork. There are no rules!"

She seems to think that she is agreeing with me while saying the opposite of what I am trying to communicate. "That's not quite true." I respond, "There are quite a lot of rules and techniques to learn."

"Those little fingers are so cute when they are all covered with paint."

Now, we *never* do finger painting in my classroom. However, I choose to keep quiet about this, because I can tell that I could spend the next hour trying to get my point across.

Why would I tell that child's mother that she was wrong, that art wasn't all about being *creative*? Surely art is just *creativity*!

I tell children and parents and that mother that she's mistaken for one reason: her five-year-old will one day be a sixth grader.

To show you what I mean, let me tell you about a fictional school where the children go to music class. When they arrive they are handed song sheets and musical instruments. Some of the children are on woodwind instruments, others on brass. A couple of kids are on percussion. One kid gets a triangle.

"Okay, students," the teacher announces, "today, we are going to learn to play some new instruments. For the next thirty minutes, I want you to just *be creative* with them. Play whatever you want."

The room is filled with noise and chaos. The teacher is

wearing her noise-canceling headphones. At the end of thirty minutes, the children have not learned to play their instruments. They have simply made noise.

The next day, the children are sent to the gym. The coach has laid out kick balls, tennis rackets, some bowling pins, and a few hockey sticks.

Coach blows the whistle. "All right, students, start playing!"

"What game are we playing, coach?" a student asks.

"Doesn't matter! *Just be creative* with the equipment."

The gym is in anarchy. One child goes to the nurse's office when he gets slapped in the face with a hockey stick.

In math class, the students are studying fractions. The room is filled with protractors, compasses, rulers, and even an abacus (which none of the students have seen before).

"Students, today we are going to *just be creative* with our math," the teacher says. "Let's explore fractions!"

Later that month, the children fail their state standardized tests and are held back a grade because they learned nothing all year. The school loses state funding, and the art department is consequently shut down. One child pulls a bead off the abacus and sticks it up his nose and has to go to the nurse's office.

You didn't attend a school like this, and neither did I. But for most people, the art room exists in this alternate universe where creativity is the only thing that matters. It sounds innocent enough to tell kindergartners to just go crazy and be creative with crayons and glue. But eventually those kindergartners, to whom creativity comes so naturally, turn into sixth graders to whom creativity often does *not* come so freely.

2.6 **Finding Our Limitations**

I have to set kids straight, tell them that art is not just about creativity, because of the second loss they will experience on their way to adulthood: they will realize their limitations.

By the time kindergartners have graduated five or six grades, they have become *very* self-conscious. And they have become *very* aware of their peers. And, furthermore, they have become very adept at comparing themselves to their peers.

By the time middle school hits, the difference between the creative "haves" and "have nots" is astounding. Some kids hang on to their creative drive. They have respectable skills. The kids who do not have realized they are "bad" at art. They are now embarrassed to try, because the kid sitting next to them is so much better. They no longer create simply because they take pleasure in it. They go to P.E. class and know who the athletes and nonathletes are. In music, students slowly understand who has "got it" and who does not. Slowly, children learn their limitations when it comes to intelligence, creativity, athleticism, and beauty, and they learn how to compare and rank themselves against their peers.

Essentially life becomes a competition. It's you against everyone.

The sentiment that art is just "creativity" seems harmless, even freeing to kindergartners. But over the years, that attitude actually *enslaves* kids. It makes the art room an elitist place, where only those who are naturally talented have a right to enjoy art, while the untalented sit on the outside, where there is weeping and gnashing of teeth. They are gripped by fear and embarrassment, staring at a blank paper, trying to just be "creative." It can be as intimidating and frustrating as a coach yelling at you while you try in vain to throw a basketball through a hoop. Eventually, most children come to believe that to create anything they have to be *creative.* They also come to believe that creativity is a commodity, and they do not possess it. Thus they stop attempting to create at all.

Saying that art is all about creativity achieves exactly what ten-year-old me wanted: it keeps art in the hands of the artists and leaves everyone else out.

How absurd is that?

It is as absurd as a gym in which only the athletic kids deserve to have fun. It is as absurd as a classroom in which only the smart kids deserve to learn to read or do math. It is as absurd as saying that only beautiful people deserve to fall in love and procreate, or that only rich people deserve to buy things, or that only religious people deserve to go to church.

2.7 The Eye of the Beholder

Picasso was right that all children are born artists.

They are also all born evangelists.

I have always believed that children should be allowed to express their faith in school. I have believed this *in theory.*

But the truth is that I have squelched many religious discussions in elementary school for one simple reason. Children have not yet realized that there is a *reason* religion and politics are not discussed in polite company. The reason is that polite company soon turns very *impolite.* I have not broken up religious *discussions* so much as I have stopped *holy wars* on the playground, as children loudly parrot fragments of Bible verses they have picked up from their parents or Sunday school. They remind me of some adults I've seen.

In a Christian school, Jesus might not be up for debate, but holy wars are still a reality, and that's the fault of Santa Claus.

Yes, jolly old St. Nick. Even when all the children believe the same thing about Jesus, they will find something to argue vehemently about. Every Christmas, schools everywhere are filled with little apologists, preaching the evidence of Santa, while the "enlightened" Santa atheists fire back. And I stand in the middle and tell them all to be quiet or I will personally cancel Christmas, because I have that ability.

Here's my takeaway from witnessing all these school yard crusades: no matter how hard children argue for or against Santa, no matter how hard they believe or do not believe, they cannot change the *facts* about Santa. They can change their *minds* about Santa or their *beliefs* or their *love* for Santa. But Santa remains a fact, unchanged.

Santa, as it turns out, is a lot like beauty.

If I recited that old adage, "Beauty is in the eye of the beholder," chances are the vast majority of us would agree.

However, it is just not true.

Our belief that beauty is in the eye of the beholder comes from our sense that we are entitled to our tastes and opinions, and who is to say that someone's tastes are better than another's? In our postmodern world, the prevailing worldview is that *all* worldviews are somehow true. We naturally believe that everyone's version of *truth* is equally valid. Your opinions and politics and religion are just as valid as my own.

This of course appeals to our emotions but makes no logical sense. We do not tell children that the sum of 2 + 2 is whatever they wish it to be. We do not tell children that *math* is in the eye of the beholder. But when it comes to the most important questions of life—*Why are we here? What is truth? What is beauty?*—in our postmodern sense of reason, we let go of the laws of logic and believe that everyone is equally right. And that is why we believe that everyone's version of beauty is equally beautiful. Nothing is ugly or vulgar or pornographic—if *someone* considers it beautiful.

To complicate matters, ask yourself this question: What if there is no beholder at all? What if *no one* reads a poem or looks at a painting or sings a song or eats a cake? Does the fact that there is no audience change the beauty (or deliciousness) of the creation?

If you are having trouble wrapping your brain around that, consider the more familiar question, "If a tree falls in the woods and no one is around, does it make a sound?" It sounds so profound and mysterious, but it really is not.

Of course the tree makes a sound! The tree vibrates the ground, which reverberates through the surrounding air. It is the height of human conceit to assume that a sound would not exist just because our ears are not present to hear it. The adage might as well be that *sound* is in the *ear* of the beholder. The ear may *hear* a sound, but it does not determine a sound's *existence*. The laws of physics operated for many, many years before the human mind even *considered* their existence. Or in the school yard debates over Santa's existence: Is Santa in the heart of the believer? No. The fact that a child believes or does not believe in Santa does not change any fact about him.

If everything in the universe from sound to math to Santa Claus is *not* in the eye of the beholder, then I think it is reasonable to conclude that beauty is the same. Sure, we all have our own tastes and preferences. But often we don't recognize beauty because we don't understand it. Or we fail to recognize a delicious meal because our palates are not trained correctly. There must be an *objective* source of beauty.

Even if everyone were suddenly stricken blind, any beauty in the world would remain unchanged. Beauty is not a purely subjective quality, different for every beholder. It is an objective quality, inherent to some things and utterly missing from others.

You may be resisting what I am telling you, but I encourage you to try to believe me, because how we think about beauty may just shape how we think of God Himself. If you ask me, the objective source for beauty happens to be the same source as truth itself. It has to be the Divine Being who created the world and all the truth and beauty it contains.

When you let go of the idea that beauty is subjective and in the eye of the beholder, you may remember that no one has ever beheld God. Yet He is no less beautiful because of that. In fact, God has told people that we could not even *handle* beholding how beautiful He is! God was beautiful long before humans were around to reflect on His beauty. He was forgiving before there were sins to forgive. He was loving before there was anyone to love. He was truth before there were liars. He was wise before there were fools.

Ancient people made sacrifices to gods, believing that their worship somehow fed or kept their god alive, that their god depended on their worship. The Aztecs believed their god relied on a constant source of human hearts. The same thinking was held by the ancient people of the Near East, whether they sacrificed food, animals, or humans. But the God of the Bible, Yahweh, vehemently denies this is the case for Himself again and again. If every Israelite forgot the covenant they had made with God, stopped speaking His name, and never worshiped Him again, God would still be who He is, and nothing less. If beauty depended on a beholder, then God's beauty and glory would be dependent on us, His creation. And dependent on us is one thing God certainly is not.

Beauty is not in the eye of the beholder.

Truth is not in the mind of the thinker.

God is not in the heart of the worshiper.

They are facts. And they need no beholder to validate them.

Sometimes, beautiful things are not recognized by more than just one or two people. That doesn't make them less beautiful. And sometimes, very unbeautiful things are extraordinarily popular, and held up as standards for beauty. But idolizing an ugly thing never imparts beauty to it. Our fickle tastes and darkened minds do not *determine* beauty. We are only fortunate if we recognize it when we see it.

It turns out that this little white lie, that beauty is in the eye of the beholder, might be the thing that hurts kids most as they grow up.

2.8 **Motivated to Be Lazy**

"Tell me what's *bad* about your art today," I say.

"These flowers aren't so good."

"I got sloppy with the paint."

"This giraffe looks like a toilet."

"Good," I say. "What else went wrong?"

Maybe it seems strange to make young children critique themselves in front of their peers. Maybe you think I am a cruel and heartless man who crushes the spirits and drinks the tears of little children. After all, we believe that all children's art is special and beautiful. It seems harsh and counterintuitive to temper praise with criticism. "Beauty is in the eye of the beholder!" you say.

Of course if we are being honest, we know that some art is good and some art is bad. Just like some math problems are wrong and some basketballs miss the hoop. But artwork is not returned to kids with red check marks like math homework, telling them what they did wrong. So art again lives in this seemingly parallel universe where all things are good and beautiful and we should let children believe that, even though it is a lie.

Why is it so terrible to believe that beauty is in the eye of the beholder? Because of the third thing that happens to us as we grow up:

We get lazy.

We lose that childish lack of self-consciousness. We discover what we're good at and what we're not so good at. And as soon as we discover our limitations, it colors how we engage with the world for the rest of our lives.

Maybe you were a talented student, but that doesn't mean

you weren't a *lazy* student too. I was the same way. I knew *exactly* how hard I had to work to get the grade I wanted, and I worked *exactly* that hard. No more, no less. In college, I perfected the art of slacking by exact percentage points. I knew exactly how long I could sleep in, how many assignments I could skip, how much I could phone it in and still get an A. I could have done better. But no one knew the difference. Teachers still called me a great student.

A talented student may come into my room and only be giving me 80 percent of her effort. How would I know the difference?

I also discovered what I was *not* good at. I was not good at playing basketball. So I quickly gave up. After all, why would I continue to make a fool of myself in front of my peers when I clearly lacked talent? Some of us figured it out sooner than others. We decided that the only things worth doing were the things we were already good at. And in the activities we were already good at, we didn't need to actually work because that is what talent is for.

But why do we excuse laziness just because we lack talent? When I hit freshman algebra, I discovered I was not *talented* at algebra. Did my teacher say, "Oh well, this isn't your thing. Just put your head down on your desk"?

No.

My lack of talent meant I had to try *harder* to get the results I desired.

I might have actually surprised myself if I had stuck with basketball. After all, I did learn algebra eventually. I stuck with learning the trumpet for two years and became decent, with no real musical *talent*.

But when we say that beauty is simply in the eye of the beholder, we give students a false lesson about the world. We teach them that there is *no* standard for success. We teach them that *their perspective* is the only measure of their life. My judgment (or for that matter, *God's* judgment) on them doesn't matter, as long as *they* are satisfied with their life.

Once this attitude takes root, it gives growth to low standards and laziness in students. *Who cares what the teacher thinks, as long as I am satisfied? Why should I strive to meet the teacher's demands? Why do God's standards matter if I am happy?*

It is a lot easier to be satisfied in life when you have low standards. It is easy to be lazy. We learn to stick with what we are already good at, avoid what we are not good at, and try to steer clear of looking foolish and taking risks. We learn to have low expectations for ourselves. We learn low standards and laziness and the defiant attitude that *no one* can judge me or try to hold me to a higher standard.

It is a new school year. We are just a few weeks in. I have spent the summer planning a great new year, preparing the room, unpacking new supplies. I am excited and ready to go.

A child approaches me with her project.

"I'm finished, Mr. Appling!" she says.

I am excited to see the child's work. She is one of my more enthusiastic students. As I look at her work though, I become a little disappointed. The project is scribbly and rushed and lazy looking. I look at the clock. She has used less than half of the allotted time. I point around on the page at the improvements I'd like her to make. She scowls and acts put upon to be asked to do more art *in art class.*

I am sad to see this happen. It is the degradation of a formerly great art student. It is not unlike witnessing the slow decline and death of a loved one. Gradually, her creative drive is atrophying. She is discovering her boundaries. And she is now satisfied with laziness, even balking at requests for additional effort. I know the pattern now, so I am not surprised. I had just hoped that I would have more time before it happened to her. I am guessing that in a couple of years, I will get a call from her mother, complaining that her child used to love art class.

It will happen to many of these students, eventually. The excited youngsters will start to show signs of creative decay by second grade; third grade, if I can help delay it. But for many of my students, I am like a doctor only able to give palliative care. This creative "sickness" that infects students is terminal, and there is no vaccine that I know of. I can try to stay positive. I can do the most fun projects I know of. I can preach to them about the importance of doing their best. I can enjoy the time I have with them as much as possible. But for many of them, I am only postponing the inevitable. The artists inside them are dying.

This is the sad burden of the art teacher, which I never considered until I stepped into the classroom. Picasso was right. Children are all born artists. Artists are not *created.* They are *born.*

But most child artists have very short life spans. Art teachers work very hard to grow and nurture as many child artists as possible. But we watch most of them simply grow up and disappear. How many artists will be lost this year? Only a few will escape into adulthood with their creativity alive.

2.9 Three Phases

In this chapter, I outlined three things that happen to every child on their way to adulthood.

Creating stopped being important. It does not matter what you created as a child. I am not just referring to art. Bit by bit, other priorities took over.

We learned our limitations. We stopped doing activities based on our enjoyment or a desire to share our creations with others and started engaging in activities based on how our peers saw us. Our interactions became based on avoiding embarrassment.

We got lazy. We hoped that talent would be a ticket to easy street, and we took our shortcomings as an excuse to stop trying. We developed low expectations for ourselves to avoid disappointment and our tolerance for risk withered.

And now you and I are adults. We have spent a lifetime learning these three attitudes, practicing them, and making them everyday instinctual habits that shape how most of us engage with the world every day. Our inner child artists have been painted over, whitewashed, covered up under many years and layers of paint. Perhaps you do not even remember that he or she ever existed.

Those three habits are what you have to shed if you are ever going to rediscover what five-year-old you knew by heart.

CREATIVE GIANTS Jim Henson

Throughout the book you will find these reflections on "creative giants." Who are they? Adults who held on to their childhood drive to create and made an impact on the world in a special way with their gifts. Everyone has creative giants in their lives. I chose these people specifically because they made my own childhood richer and more beautiful in their own ways. As you read about these men and women, reflect on the adults who made your childhood a bit more beautiful.

JIM HENSON (1936–1990): Henson was a puppeteer and a skilled and visionary designer. Prior to Henson, puppets were typically made of wood, were controlled with strings, and had seemingly random facial movements. Henson revolutionized the art of puppet making by believing that puppets should have lives and souls that communicate to people. He constructed puppets out of foam rubber and developed many other advances in puppeteering to make characters more expressive and emotive. The result of Henson's vision for a world of living puppets is the most creative, well-researched, and longest running educational children's show ever, *Sesame Street*. In addition, *The Muppet Show* was the most watched show *of all* at the time. Henson left behind a revolutionized art form, an army of fans. His most famous muppet, Kermit the Frog (one of his older incarnations, at least), now rests in the Smithsonian Institute.

Of course, Henson's vision would never have reached millions of children without the work of visionaries around him. Joan Ganz Cooney was a television producer who pioneered early research on the potential of television to educate children. She founded the Children's Television Workshop, which made *Sesame Street* possible.

2.10 Good or Good Enough

"Are you a biscuit?" I ask a student.

"What?" The student looks at me, confused.

The student is clearly not a biscuit or any kind of baked good for that matter. I just remember one of my crotchety old teachers always asking that question of me. I now use the question to combat one of the most oft-repeated statements in the classroom: "I'm done."

My teacher's goal was to get us to say that we were "finished" rather than "done." I don't care so much about grammar as the fact that we have forty-five minutes of an hour-long class left, and this student's artwork looks like a cat threw up on his paper, and he's smiling proudly, like he just won a Nobel Prize.

I make some suggestions about how the student can make his work look less cat vomity, and send him back to his seat. Thirty seconds later, he returns.

"I'm done."

Again, I send him back to his seat because his work has made no discernible progress in the extra half minute of "work."

We repeat this dance five times over the next few minutes.

"What should I do now?" the student asks.

I almost can't believe it. Something has clicked in the student's head and my own.

I make an announcement. "Kids, from now on, I never want to hear any of you tell me 'I'm done.' Those two words are banned forever. Master artists never say they are done. A master artist instead asks, 'What can I do to make this work better?'"

The next week, there's a new poster on the wall with the new phrase: *How Can I Make My Project Better?* I haven't heard the forbidden words since then.

It is not just that students saying, "I'm done," or the popular alternative, "Is this good?" annoyed me as a teacher. It is that those two phrases are terrible habits. When a student tells me they are done, it is because they want to quit. When a student asks, "Is this good?" they are telling me the same thing. If they get my approval, then they feel justified in quitting.

They are not really asking me, "Is this good?"

They are asking me, "Is this good *enough*?"

Asking a question like "Is this good?" is a habit that starts popping up at the tender age of six or seven. The question indicates that the wheels on the student's creative drive are starting to rust. They are no longer being generous with their creativity but instead are starting to live within their perceived limitations. They are being tempted to settle for laziness. They are starting to set low standards for themselves.

And that question becomes a way of life. It is probably how you live your life without even thinking about it.

"Is this good enough?"

Living life by "good enough" wraps up all the things we lost as we grew up. You can summarize this whole chapter with that question: "Is this good enough?" When you give up creating, live by your limitations, and stop being generous with your talents, you are living merely "good enough."

If you are living by "good enough," then you are living life at the bare minimum, by low standards. "Good enough" is about survival and nothing more. "Good enough" forfeits control of your life to the judgment of others. "Good enough" assumes that the "goodness" of life is in the eye of the beholder. "Good enough" is a lazy standard and it makes people miserable.

If you are living life by a "good enough" philosophy, then you are living like a teenager who only tries to get a passing grade or a worker trying to do just enough to not get fired. You will never discover your true potential at "good enough." You will never exceed expectations at "good enough." You will never surprise yourself at "good enough." And no one will be more hurt than you by "good enough."

In math class, you could not improve on a "right" answer. Right answers were "good enough." You could not come up with a "better" answer, or exceed the teacher's expectations.

Life is not like math class. It is like art class. In the next chapters, we'll talk about living a "good" life, rather than a "good enough" life.

QUESTIONS FOR THOUGHT

1. *When did creating things begin to have less of a priority in your life? What became more important? Where does creating rank on your list of priorities today?*

2. *When did you discover your limitations—that you weren't good at sports or art or music or math? What was the last new activity that you were willing to try, even if it meant failing?*

3. *When did you become self-conscious and fearful of your limitations? What are you unwilling to do today because "it will never work"?*

CHAPTER THREE

Life without *BEAUTY*

society suffers an epidemic of lost creativity

3.1 Happy Little Trees

When I was born in the early eighties, my parents were living in a tiny house provided by a tiny church, in a tiny Ozark town. Dad was the pastor of the Methodist church and Mom was an elementary schoolteacher. As you might guess, a small town pastor and schoolteacher do not make a lot of money. Despite this, they prepared for my birth with a major purchase.

Prior to my emergence into the world, their living room was furnished with a thirteen-inch black-and-white television set. It had an ugly yellow plastic casing and a handle on top. Since this was the early eighties, *Sesame Street* was dominating children's educational programming. My parents would not hear of their little boy watching *Sesame Street*, attempting to learn his shapes and colors, on a black-and-white television. So along with a rocking chair and a crib, they brought home a twenty-one-inch Zenith color set, complete with beautiful faux wood casing.

While *Sesame Street* was the reason for the purchase of the new television, I found a much more personal companion in Bob Ross, who hosted *The Joy of Painting*. Every episode of Ross's show was essentially the same: paint a serene landscape, complete with puffy clouds and happy little trees, with some very simple techniques.

Bob Ross had an unmistakably quiet demeanor and a perfectly calm, soothing voice. When I read in the Bible that Elijah heard God as a "still, small voice," I wonder if God's voice sounded like Bob Ross. His personality would be enough to lull most kids to sleep (and made *Mister Rogers' Neighborhood* look like epilepsy-inducing Japanese anime by comparison), but he captured my imagination. I pantomimed right along with Bob Ross, holding my invisible palette, painting on my invisible canvas, and beating the devil out of my invisible brushes, just like he jokingly told us to do, every episode. Bob Ross was my art teacher until I went off to school.

At about the age of twelve, the "still, small voice" began to speak to me again. In my bedroom, I collected a few supplies, set up an old box that I took camping, and began once again to channel my inner Bob Ross. I painted dozens and dozens of landscapes full of puffy clouds and happy trees. While some boys might have been secretly lifting weights in their bedrooms, I was gradually building up my technique and confidence with a brush.

I also repeatedly spilled paint on my bedroom carpet while

working, a habit that disgusted my mother. She did eventually forget this sin—when she discovered that I was also blowing out my trumpet's spit valve onto my bedroom carpet. Did she want me to get good at playing the trumpet or waste valuable practice time constantly walking to the bathroom to blow spit into the sink? You can't have both, Mom.

3.2 Unnecessary Creation

A child's desire to create something new or a soft-spoken man's teaching children and adults how to paint may seem innocent and innocuous but not *necessary* to the survival or advancement of the human race. It may be easy to assume that in times and places where life is difficult and human survival is tenuous, that people do *not* spend their time in such frivolous, unnecessary pursuits as *creating*.

You may assume that prehistoric man was too occupied with finding food that he would not have had the time, energy, or perhaps even *insight* to exercise any creativity. But your assumption would be wrong. Creativity is a timeless, even *primal*, urge and seems to undergird every activity that humans have ever engaged.

Thousands of years ago, give or take a few, when people had to do more to find their supper than go to the grocery store, a handful of men were on the hunt. They had been away from their homes and families, tracking animals for days. They had a few provisions, but they were hungry, thirsty, and tired. Their weapons were ready to strike. If they did not make this kill, their tiny community might not survive the next season.

And at some point during the hunt, one of the men decided to commemorate or invoke a blessing for the hunt with some art, a painting on the wall of a cave.

Several of these cave paintings, many thousands of years old, have turned up around the world. They depict hunts and ceremonies and other illustrations of daily life for ancient humanity. The caves are sacred spaces. Unlike ordinary settlements, the caves lack trash and other evidence of human activity. It seems that even ancient man kept his art in museums and places of prayer. The paintings were revisited and revised many times by these ancient people.

Hunting is serious business. The survival of those prehistoric people depended on it. Yet someone took the time to create something beautiful. Isn't that amazing?

The Denver Art Museum features a gallery of the art of Native Americans from the Pacific Northwest region. You might think a hunter in one of these tribes would select the most basic of hunting tools. After all, hunting is a dirty, gritty, bloody, primal affair. It doesn't happen in an art museum. But instead, a tribal craftsman spent hours fashioning exquisitely beautiful knives, arrows, and other tools. Creating a beautiful object for the hunt was a spiritual exercise, a sign of respect and reverence for the animal whose life was taken to sustain human life.

The little caption with the tools explained that, in the words of one tribesman, the spirit of the hunted animal "prefers to be killed by a beautiful object." I don't know if animals have preferences about how they will be killed. But the sheer *unneces-sary* beauty of the hunting tools is amazing. The amount of time and effort the artisans spent making the tools, when they could have been *actually hunting*, is astounding.

The respect those hunters showed to the craft makes me look at my plain old kitchen knives with a bit of disdain. *"Be more beautiful!"* I bark at the knives, as I slice some tomatoes.

The tomatoes also resent being butchered by such ugly knives but suffer this indignity without saying so.

Consider now the masters of Renaissance art, many genera-tions later, who also happened to be some of the world's foremost *scientists*. Renaissance artists became obsessed with realistic depictions of the natural world. Artists spent lifetimes study-ing linear perspective (how objects disappear and converge as they move farther from the eye). Human anatomy was rigorously documented for the first time, as artists secured human cadavers for dissection.

The mysterious phenomenon of light was meticulously cal-culated. Do you know why the most realistic paintings of people look so realistic? Artists realized that human skin is translu-cent, allowing light to penetrate and be reflected back, making it "glow." A Renaissance (or, more likely, Baroque) artist with a keen eye for light would paint human skin in multiple layers of very thin paint, allowing the light to actually *penetrate* the paint, hit the canvas underneath, and be reflected back through the paint to the viewer's eye, where the paint appeared to glow with a natural luminosity. These artists were true masters who used scientific knowledge to enhance the beauty they were able to create. Much like in the case of the hunters, creativity appears to be something of an *instinct* that people follow, whatever circumstances they live in.

In college, my friends and I would gather at a dingy upstairs joint on Tuesday nights. We didn't go for the atmosphere. The place was a shabby hole in the wall with broken windows, bare lightbulbs, and wobbly tables that would spill any drink placed on them. Nor did we go for the possibility of meeting women. No woman would show up to this kind of place unescorted.

We went for the jazz music.

For three hours, we could listen to a dozen or more guys play big band jazz. Through music, we were transported to a much different time. All that was missing was Tommy Dorsey or Glenn Miller. The audience was usually no bigger than the band itself, and we paid no cover charge. These guys were just here, in this dingy place, playing outdated music on Tuesday nights. And they weren't making a dime for it. Does that not sound like a huge waste of time and energy?

I took my wife there on one of our first dates. And I have kept a collection of jazz records ever since.

The cave paintings and the Renaissance masters, the hunters and jazz musicians. What does it all *mean*?

Human life is an exceptionally complicated endeavor. Just being born is difficult and painful and messy. And from there, it only gets tougher. For thousands of years, the odds of surviving childhood were quite low. Human life consisted of the dangerous work of hunting animals or the tedious labor of subduing the land for agriculture.

Humans have always had their hands full when it comes to just surviving. You would think we'd live purely *functional* lives. The animals do it this way. They dig holes and build nests to live in. The animals live lives of utilitarian function and minimalism. If humans wanted to, we could have a similar existence. We could fashion only the most functional clothing. We could build only the most basic huts for the sole purpose of providing the barest shelter. We could live our lives only on the most basic necessities of food, shelter, and procreation.

But the stories of human creation I just shared with you—the hunting tools, the cave paintings, the Renaissance masters, the jazz music—all seem to flaunt the difficulty and complication of human life. Humans have never lived purely functional lives, even when life was *most* difficult, when our survival was most precarious. We are *compelled* to create. Humans mysteriously create things with no practical function or purpose other than to be *beautiful*. Humans prepare to hunt by fashioning beautiful tools. Humans make music that disappears into the air as soon as it is created. Almost nothing in our lives, from our living spaces to our bodies to the world around us, escapes our attention as we leave our mark on it. No animal does this.

Why do humans? Why are we driven to create things, to re-create our world as we see fit? Here is the reason: *In the book of Genesis, God created the universe.*

And when God created the universe, He filled it with billions of stars, which I imagine humans will never see. He has created endless wonders that we will never discover. Throughout the universe, trillions of sunrises and sunsets happen with no one to enjoy them, except for God Himself. You may call the universe a rather excessive bit of creative opulence. Whoever needed a universe *so* big and beautiful? Apparently God loves creating beauty enough that He just could not help Himself, even knowing that no one would ever see it. (Because God knows that beauty is not in the eye of the beholder.)

When God was finished creating this big, beautiful, unnecessary universe, with all of its excessive glory and gratuitous beauty, the thought occurred to Him that He should make a race of people in His own image.

In His *own image* . . .

I suspect humanity's drive to create is one of the keys to what it means to be "made in the image of God." The same drive for creating that God has in His heart, He placed in the first human heart.

It is that divine drive that left paintings on the walls of caves thousands of years ago. That human *compulsion* crafted thousands of tiny, delicate sculptures and grand wonders. The godly DNA inside us compels us to engineer complex musical instruments or choreograph dances or write dramas and poems.

Human survival never demanded that a poem be written or a song be sung or a play be performed or a story be told or any number of other beautiful, emotional, moving things be created. *Beauty* is never essential to survival. Yet humanity has spent *millions* of hours on *unnecessary, nonessential creation.*

God's life is not just about *existing.* It is about *beauty.* And when God made human life, He made it to be not just about survival. Human life, in God's mind, is about beauty and purpose and pleasure and recreation and love. We are uniquely fashioned to experience all of these things. It is why people work jobs they love even though the pay is weak or entertain hobbies or explore the unknown or get married or go to church or paint a painting.

3.3 Art Is Forsaken

Yes, history is replete with evidence of humanity's creative abilities, evidence of our reflection of our Divine Creator. This divine drive has benefitted and enriched humanity since our very beginning. It has expressed all of our passions that words cannot. Humanity can accomplish great things *when we retain our God-given creative drives.*

However, as we discussed, kids grow up and most forget about creating. Sure, it is probably no big deal if *one* sixth grader gives up being creative and embraces lazy, "good enough" living. It is probably not going to affect us even if *many* sixth graders live this way, as they let their inner artists die. But what would our society look like if our naturally born creativity was *completely* forgotten and forsaken, on a widespread scale, like an epidemic?

I think we are living that reality right now.

I look around at our twenty-first-century society and it makes me wonder if *the whole world* has forgotten about creating. The problem of one sixth grader giving up creativity has become an epidemic. I wonder if we as an entire generation are not losing touch with our creative natures. Have we lost that essential component of our human DNA? Modern society presents symptoms that lead me to believe that we have.

It was not too long ago that people still appreciated creativity. The Renaissance brought the world out of the Dark Ages. Science and art and every human endeavor were in revival. The church was the world's foremost patron of the arts. The church was *creating* culture.

How things have changed over such a short time.

I find some measure of irony in teaching art in a Christian school, considering how the relationship between Christian culture and creativity has changed so drastically since the days of the Renaissance. Where once, the church generated and patronized the greatest artistic geniuses of the time, today it may be difficult to identify the creative masters in our midst. Faith and creativity formerly were inextricably intertwined. Today, faith and art often seem at odds. Vast swaths of modern Christianity seem to be completely removed from creative pursuits, and likewise the vast world of art is often devoid of the influence of people of faith. Certainly a few brave people continue to express their faith through timeless traditions of creativity. But just as certainly, much of the creative energy in the name of faith amounts to nothing more than making T-shirts that riff on pop culture trends.

Is the canon of *great* Christian art closed?

The modern separation of church and art pits two natural human tendencies—worship and creativity—at odds with one another. The two should go hand in hand, as they did for millennia. Whatever the reason, the compartmentalizing of art and faith has made an enormous impact on modern living, and contributed to our often unbeautiful, uncreative existence. Now, the church is patron to neither art nor science, and sometimes not even faith.

Consider, too, the ubiquitous modern worldview. Our own minds have been trained to shun creative living.

Today, people are exceptionally modern-minded. We worship Darwin, and believe life is just a series of mere circumstances. We bow to Freud and believe life is just sex. We meditate on the sacred texts of the self-help section at the bookstore and believe that life is just a formula. We don't admit any of these habits. It is just so ingrained in us that it comes without thinking about it.

It is a strange, completely modern experiment that we are conducting. Can we reduce life to purely *utilitarian* functions, to a *formula*? If I follow these five steps, can I *conquer* life? It is a way of viewing ourselves, our life, our world, and our God that has never occurred to the heart of man before.

Christians like to believe that we are separate from the world, that modern, humanist, postmodern worldviews do not affect us. However, I think even our ancient Christian faith has been profoundly reshaped by our disastrous separation from beauty and creativity.

How so? It's all about how we read the Bible.

When God created us, He knew that all of our scientific

endeavors would answer many questions. But He also knew that our science would not answer our most important questions about *purpose* or *truth*. Those are the questions that keep a human awake at night, gripped in the fear that his life is a waste and without purpose or importance.

So God, in an effort to calm those fears, revealed the answer. But He did it in a very *unscientific, unmodern,* but very *beautiful* way. The Bible is a book that is full of all manner of human drama: love, loss, poetry, song, humor, sex, drunkenness, and everything else humans do. Maybe God planned it that way

 ## CREATIVE GIANTS Edwin Binney

EDWIN BINNEY (1866–1934): Most people probably do not think immediately of businessmen as the most creative guys around. But why not? When people think of the most creative companies of the twenty-first century, they think of revolutionary companies like Apple and the creative giant behind the brand, Steve Jobs.

Edwin Binney wasn't quite the Steve Jobs of his time. But his products have had a far longer shelf life than any Apple product so far. His little company started out making industrial colorants,

which still doesn't sound too creative. But from those products, Binney had a vision. He saw a need in the market, specifically among children, and he converted his business to meet that need. He began manufacturing wax crayons, packed in little boxes, for children to use at school in a time when crayons were expensive artists' tools. Combining two French words, his wife, Alice, named the little crayons "crayola."

See what I mean? You do not have to be "creative" in the traditional sense to create something great to share with the world.

because He knew that He'd need to keep our attention somehow, and since God is all-knowing, He knows that sex sells.

In all seriousness, the Bible reads this way because the deepest questions and longings of the human heart cannot be answered with *formulas.*

But it is our foolish, scientific, modern minds that look past the beauty, literary grace and variety of the Bible, the mystery of the gospel, the majesty of God's revelation, and demand that it all function as a science textbook. It is precisely that ultramodern thinking that causes most Christians to miss the truth of the Bible, many other Christians to become disaffected with the Bible, and non-Christians to scoff at the Bible. We are stripping all the beauty out of the Bible and demanding that it provide us with a *formula* instead of *faith.*

3.4 Life without Beauty

We live in a time when we seriously risk stripping all of the creative beauty from our faith. And our modern mindset is trained to reject beauty and embrace formulaic thinking. But even everyday living has very little beauty today, beauty that used to be commonplace. Most of us do not even know what we are missing.

My wife and I have an annual tradition of touring some of the homes in the oldest neighborhood of our city around Christmastime. They range from century-old Queen Anne homes to humble postwar bungalows. It is amazing to see the beauty and charm that used to come standard with buying even an average home. Stained-glass windows, grand staircases, elaborate woodwork, deco-styled heat registers were common-place. Even modest homes were given unique touches. And this was before people had heard of granite countertops, double vanities, or other modern "necessities."

And then we drive home through the modern suburbs. The homes are not built for beauty anymore. Much like the produce in your grocery store is not farmed primarily for taste or nutrition but for durability in shipping, homes are now produced with efficiency of construction and square footage being the primary goals. Even guys who lived in caves felt the need to dress the place up with some art. But so many modern neighborhoods are remarkable for their remarkable uniformity.

How did the American neighborhood see such a radical transformation in just a few decades? Like most things that are forfeited, we gave up beautiful neighborhoods bit by bit, while hardly noticing.

Take, as a small example, those grand front porches that greet the visitors of homes built a century ago. The front porch was a thing of beauty, a welcoming space where neighbors were received. It was an extra living space for the residents. It promoted socializing with neighbors and passers-by. The front porch was the dominate feature of a modern home a hundred years ago, and it defined American hospitality.

Henry Ford changed all that, though he did not know it or intend to.

When everyone in the neighborhood bought a car, they needed a place to store their cars. Homeowners and developers began building garages onto the backs of homes. Alleys connected driveways, and the front yards and porches were left pristine and welcoming.

But eventually, city planning caught up, as government bureaucracies always do. People decided that alleys were unsafe. They were filled with trash cans. They were narrow and dark, and people no longer wanted them. The reasonable solution was to ban the use of alleys, and developers began building homes with front-facing garages. The dominate feature of a modern American home is no longer a large, welcoming front porch but car storage; a big box where people keep their cars and their junk. The profound effect this simple change had on American life is staggering. I *never* sit in front of my home, greeting my neighbors as they pass by.[1]

The example of porches and garages is just one of a million little bits of everyday beauty that our modern culture has traded away, most of us without even being aware it is happening. Many of us travel to jobs and sit in ugly cubicles. We stare out the car window at ugly billboards. The waiting rooms of the world are filled with mass-produced art. We fill our stomachs with mass-produced food. Doesn't real beauty seem *unusual*?

People underestimate the power of aesthetics. The spaces we create for living, for work, for play, or for worship profoundly shape those activities we engage in and how we feel about those activities, and we are spending a great deal of our time in ugly spaces.

3.5 The Ugliness Inside

But none of those things even compare to the *human* ugliness we are soaked in from day to day. Our nightly news is full of ugliness and hate. Marriages are filled with ugliness until they end prematurely. Our culture is deeply and vehemently divided over petty issues. The powers of the world constantly threaten one another. Greed seems to poison every pure endeavor. The sex industry enslaves millions. People are estranged and alienated and cruel, even to people they say they love. Americans consume the most antidepressants of any culture, and yet we still feel terrible.

Why? Because the ugliness that can be found in the human heart far exceeds the ugliness we can build around us.

Every once in a while, we are touched profoundly by the ugliness that humanity is capable of creating.

One day in my college years, I sat in a Mexican restaurant. One of the booths was nearly filled with guys about my age, enjoying their food, when they were approached by another young man. The newcomer had a debilitating speech impediment, and it was apparent that he dealt with other serious physical maladies. His limitations made him the subject of speculation, but not of friendship.

It was obvious that the young men at the table knew him. They exchanged short greetings.

The newcomer asked if he could sit.

Implicit in this simple question was the underlying question: *Will you accept me as your equal, as your peer, as a man, as a human?*

The table fell into awkward silence. One guy took the lead, explaining that the table was full, which was not true. He made the newcomer with the speech impediment stand there alone. He remained an outsider as he was sent away. I imagine he was not unused to this treatment. Whatever his disabilities, he was fully cognizant of having been rejected by his peers and insulted as a man.

My faced burned as I observed this . . . because I was sitting at the table that turned him away. To my shame, I said nothing. I kept quiet as the newcomer turned around and left to sit alone. It is perhaps the ugliest thing I have ever participated in, the fifteen or twenty seconds of my life I am still most ashamed of so many years later.

Every once in a while, we are touched profoundly by the ugliness that humanity is capable of creating, because we realize that we don't have to turn on the news to see it. We don't have to blame others for it. We, too, are just as capable of creating it.

3.6 Timelessness

It is difficult for me as a relatively young, twenty-first-century American to contemplate how *old* some things are. America is a relatively young nation. For thousands of years, our whole continent was covered with an ocean that deposited all the little fossilized crinoids that my childhood friend and I would one day find in a creek bed. When the waters receded, trees covered the Midwestern landscape for centuries more. And about fifty years ago, some of the trees were cleared and my neighborhood was built. Fifty years sounds pretty old, doesn't it?

I was a child when I first visited the Nelson Atkins Museum of Art in Kansas City. Since then, I have visited many times. It is a grand neoclassical building, a labyrinth of quiet, dimly lit rooms. There is a feeling and a *smell* to places like this that give them a sense of spirituality.

I recall seeing what amounted to an ancient Chinese doll-house on my first visit. The house was intricately decorated, with the seemingly superhuman patience and skill that Asian craftsmen take pride in and Americans often cannot understand. The plaque told visitors that the house was thought to be from the first century.

I was in awe. How could something be so *old*?

As a child, I misunderstood the meaning of "first century" and believed that the house was practically from the beginning of human existence. Little did I realize that the first century was just the first century A.D., and there were actually quite a few centuries prior to that. There were things in the world that were *much* older and more inspiring than the dollhouse.

But I still remember that dollhouse because it was my first, profound realization of *time*. How could it be that a man in a place I have never visited, in a time I cannot imagine, speaking a language I cannot speak, could create something so beautiful that it would survive *two thousand years* after its creator's death, and be looked upon by a know-nothing, eight-year-old boy?

That is what is called *timeless*.

Art museums are full of timelessness. A gulf may divide the viewers from the artists, a gulf made of time, culture, language, and beliefs. We'd have virtually nothing in common with the man or woman who created the art. But when we go a museum and put on that little visitor badge and sit on the little bench, we are bound to a person long ago and far away by what he created. The art is *timeless*. It will always be beautiful. It will always say something about the craftsman, about the culture he lived in, about his mind and heart.

I sincerely doubt that people any time soon will grow tired of filing past the *Mona Lisa*. It is just a modestly sized portrait of an unknown woman. But it is *timeless*. Michelangelo's *David* is just a chunk of marble, made to look less like an Israelite shepherd and more like a Greek god with enormous hands. Today, the ankles of the statue have dozens of microcracks, resulting from the vibrations of nearby trains. Experts are scrambling to preserve David. But even if David's ankles shatter and he has to be propped up on a stick, he will be no less timeless or glorious.

Things that are timeless are striking because they contrast so vividly with our everyday experience.

My life does not look like an art museum. It is not full of timeless things that will survive my death, which people will look on in wonder for centuries. It is hard for me to imagine that *anyone* today is creating anything that will be remembered.

Instead of timeless things, my world is full of *disposable* things. My commute to work is cluttered with advertisements for junk I should not buy. My cable subscription is full of junk I should not watch. The bookstore is full of junk I should not read. And if that's not enough, my Internet connection can provide an endless supply of junk I should not look at. It all has an incredibly short shelf life, and very little of it is really, timelessly beautiful.

It is difficult to find the good, beautiful, timeless stuff among the junk.

Junk is manufactured constantly, nonstop, twenty-four hours a day. But why?

3.7 Even the Playground

"Mr. Appling, come see what we found!"

I am walking across the playground at my first full-time job as a teacher's aide. I am accompanied by a few third graders, and I can tell whatever a kid found on the other side of the yard isn't going to be good.

I can see from a distance a kid pulling some flat rectangular object from the big puddle. The big puddle is always there, and it is always a temptation. We tell the kids every day to stay out of the big puddle. But now they've found buried treasure, so there's no way we'll be able to keep them away from it. They are going to constantly be fishing in the gunk for more treasure.

And there it is.

The kid has pulled a porn magazine from the puddle. Awesome.

And look, there's a second one still laying in the water, pages stuck together. I hear the word "sex" being whispered. Even though the kids are hazy on the particulars of sex, they know that this is "sex."

I snatch the magazines from the boy's hand and walk in a decidedly hurried manner toward the recycling bin.

"Mr. Appling, are you taking those magazines *home*?" the boy shouts at me.

"No!" I bark back. "And don't you dare tell anyone I am either!"

Even after I escape the barrage of billboards on my commute to work and try to avoid most of the other junk being peddled to me, even the safe enclave of a school playground can't be kept pristine from the ugliness that human adults produce. Even if a kid's computer has every filter and parental lock on it, pornography will somehow find itself in a puddle on a school yard for the kid to pick up.

3.8 Beauty or Profit

The sad reality is that timeless things do not create profit. Advertisements and skin magazines make profit. That is why the global junk factory is never shut down. It is why those kids found that magazine on the playground. It all makes money.

It is the way it has always been. Great art has always needed wealthy benefactors. The art you see in a museum exists because the church or a king or a wealthy patron was able to pay an artist's living expenses. Vincent Van Gogh was never able to make money on his art. His brother, Theo, continually supported the artist financially throughout his life. Vincent died penniless and mentally broken, having sold just *one* painting in his lifetime. Today his paintings are some of the most expensive that have ever been auctioned.

Perhaps it is because timeless beauty does not create wealth that our modern world, with its grand experiment of utilitarian living, does not bother too much with it.

The vast majority of our culture's artistic energies are devoted to creating advertisements to clutter the world or pop culture, which is meant to be consumed and then mentally thrown away.

An author writes a book, which she hopes will hit the bestseller list, before quickly fading into obscurity. A popular singer writes a formulaic song that will top the charts and be played several times a day by DJs everywhere. The catchy hook will be on the lips of fans. As soon as the song reaches saturation, fans will become bored and sick of the once infectious rhythm, and the song will mercifully drop off the charts and out of our airwaves.

I once heard an interview on the radio with a popular singer who described writing and rewriting a song over the course of ten—yes, *ten*—days, as if working for that long on a three-minute ditty was a notable accomplishment of dedication and willpower. The contrast between the ancient Chinese craftsman, meticulously carving tiny details, and the pop singer tweaking the auto-tuner for *ten days* is striking.

Today, most things we consume are cheap, unimportant, and disposable. The things we create have an exceptionally short shelf life and a rapidly approaching expiration date. We consume, we repeat. Consume, repeat.

We accept this, and lower our expectations.

We lower our expectations by training ourselves to *crave* the cheap, mass-produced, convenient option. We lower our expectations by listening to cheap music and eating cheap food and watching cheap entertainment and looking at cheap art and reading cheap books and believing cheap philosophies and listening to cheap sermons and having cheap faith in a cheap god.

We actually have an *epidemic*. We have an epidemic of addiction to the cheap, ugly, and disposable. We line up at the feed trough of culture and are kept alive—barely. A huge swath of the population goes through life with hands outstretched, not with an offering of anything valuable to the world but only to *take* from the world, to be *dependent* on the ugly things the world hands to it. We dull our senses to this sad reality with heavy doses of escapism. Like a drug, it takes our mind off the fact that the world we live in is quite ugly. We settle for "good enough."

How far we have come from those hunters who interrupted their bid for survival to smear paint, made of ash and blood, on a stone wall. Their lives must have been much harder and much shorter than yours or mine, but they were actually *creating* something.

That is what made them human.

Our present reality is not what we were created for. It's a sad illusion. We've traded what was intended to be our beautiful, rich, human existence for this cheap, disposable, inhuman one.

This trade we've made—the life we have for the life we could have—really is the fundamental sin of humanity. We always trade the greater thing for the lesser, the beautiful for the unbeautiful, the timeless for the *now*.

Think of Adam and Eve. God created them and placed them in a vast, lush, perfect garden. They were in absolute paradise. Their work was meaningful and fulfilling. Plus, they pranced around naked all over the place without a care in the world. They had unfettered communication with God as their Creator. Everything was *perfect*.

And they traded *everything* . . .

. . . an *entire garden* . . .

. . . *paradise* . . .

...God Himself...

...For one tree...

...one piece of fruit.

Sometime later, two brothers named Jacob and Esau had the usual brotherly rivalry. Esau was the older, and in ancient society that meant his inheritance would be double what his brother would receive when Dad died. He would be in charge of the estate and all the money. It was his birthright. He was Dad's favorite, and he let little brother, Jacob, know that every day.

Until one day when Esau was hunting and doing other very manly activities, and came home absolutely famished. Jacob was more of a momma's boy, and had been cooking with his mother that day. Esau demanded a bowl of soup from Jacob.

And Jacob seized his chance. He slyly offered a trade with big brother.

Esau made the trade. He traded his *entire future, his birthright*—for *one bowl of soup.*

Esau walked away with dinner, and Jacob walked away with his brother's life.

People have been making the same lousy trades ever since.

And now here we are in the twenty-first century, trading *real* beauty for ugliness and cheap things. That is the world we live in today. We exchange truth for lies, intimacy for images, salvation for self-help.

Remember, just because we accept and live this existence doesn't mean this is all somehow *beautiful* or *good.* We obsessively chase some standard of human beauty (and spend billions on unused gym memberships in that pursuit). That does not make our standard *beautiful*. Our culture looks at pornography constantly. That doesn't mean pornography is somehow beautiful. If every Christian were stuck in empty, false worship where their itching ears were filled with empty promises, it would not make their worship any truer, just because they accepted it. Remember, beauty is not in the eye of the beholder. There are millions of us who think we have beauty in our lives, but it turns out that we desperately need our vision checked.

3.9 What Does It Say about the Creator?

Why do people occupy themselves with digging up the past?

The *Indiana Jones* movies are probably the most popular movie franchise based on archaeology. The real world of archaeology probably has a bit less adventure (and fewer snakes). Still, digging up the past carries a certain air of intrigue and exploration that keeps attracting people, persuading them to sift through dirt and sand in search of fragments of lost civilizations.

People continue to search for the remains of our ancestors, and not just for kicks, not just to have a neat collection to show off. People dig through ancient ruins and restore artifacts and study them and display them in museums because things that are created give clues about the creator. We are searching for clues about the *people who made them*. A million little creations from eons ago are waiting to give clues about the men and women who created them.

One day I interrupted the fifth graders in their work and asked them to put down their paintbrushes. Sixty minutes is precious little time each week in an art class, and we were on the homestretch. But I suddenly had a lightning bolt moment.

I posed this question to the students: If you believe that God created the world, then what does the world say about God? After all, a creation always gives clues about its creator. People have always looked to the rocks and trees and skies and seas for clues about the divine mind behind them all.

Does the nature of the world tell us that God is rational? Logical? Chaotic? Loving? Spiteful? Meticulous? Careless? Weak? Powerful? Evil? Good?

And what, students, are your creations saying about you? When I look through a stack of your artwork, what conclusions can I make about you as students? What does the homework you turn in tell your teacher? The students pondered the question thoughtfully. Some glanced uncomfortably at their own artwork. Their paintings had become like mirrors, reflecting their hearts back at them.

When our modern culture is long gone, and we are all buried deep underground, some archaeologists from a faraway place will dig us up with all the things we created, looking for clues about our lives. What conclusions will they draw about us? After all, the things we create will tell our story, unvarnished, good or bad. We will not be around to explain ourselves in a positive light.

There is a great focus today on the amount of trash and waste that modern man produces, and we prioritize reducing waste. But think about the *mental* landfill that we've created with all of the junk that fills our minds. It dwarfs everything we throw in the trash can.

3.10 Left Behind

I have covered a lot of territory, so let's have a little review here. In chapter 2, I described the decline of the average child artist, the child who goes from "good" to striving for no more than "good enough." In this chapter, I have attempted to describe to you my vision of our culture: in the grip of an *epidemic* of lost child artists. This is our culture living life after art, without beauty or creativity.

First, we took a look at a few examples of all of the beautiful, unnecessary creation that humans have engaged in throughout our existence. It is these creative endeavors that link us to

CREATIVE GIANTS Fred Rogers

FRED ROGERS (1928–2003): Fred Rogers first saw television as a young man and completely hated it, which may not have been all that surprising, since he studied to be a Presbyterian minister. But more specifically, he hated the way television was being used to reach children. He found it demeaning and insulting to children. It was not good enough for him.

Rogers could have spent his life disdaining television, but instead he realized an endearing creative vision that affected millions of children. He developed the characters that inhabited the Neighborhood of Make-Believe, numerous songs, and a creative persona, including the trademark sneakers and cardigans in *Mister Rogers' Neighborhood* that children watched for 895 episodes.

Perhaps most important, Fred Rogers was not an actor. He did not believe in presenting a different version of himself to children on camera. He believed children could spot phonies a mile away and that one of the best gifts to be given is your own honest self.[2]

God, our Creator, and show us what we are really capable of accomplishing.

Then we saw how our modern culture is systematically deprived of real beauty and creativity, how we neglect all the unnecessary creativity that has marked the high points of humanity's past. Christian faith and worship has been divided from human creativity for centuries. Our modern minds reduce life to mere formulas, even when we read the ancient Scriptures of the Bible.

We then saw a picture of modern living conditions, an existence of mass-produced everything. Little that is made is intended to be enduring or timeless. It is meant only to be profitable and disposable: from food, to homes, to entertainment, to pornography. Worse still, we are saturated in human ugliness, and perhaps the ugliest realization a person can have is that they are just as capable of creating it as anyone else.

We considered what creations say about their creator, and I asked you to consider what our creations say about us as a people.

And now, I want to talk about hoarding.

Some people hoard material objects. They are trying to fill some void in their lives with knickknacks and other things of little value. The incredible human misery of a compulsive hoarder even makes good cable television. It is shocking to watch people living in *filth*. They are living in a worthless trash dump, a house-shaped landfill. They are miserable, *but they cannot stop or throw the trash away.*

My grandparents' house was just a bit like this. It was their retirement home. It had plenty of space for two retired folks. But it did *not* have enough space for two retired folks, *and all the junk they felt the need to keep.* Grandma was a paper pack rat. The spare rooms were stacked with boxes of receipts and letters and other miscellanea. Grandpa was a retired engineer. He was a meticulous craftsman. But he left behind a houseful of junk. Every spare nail or screw had a home in his workshop. Grandpa even hoarded food. If there was a sale on frozen orange juice concentrate, he might buy fifty cans of frozen orange juice concentrate.

Hoarding has become another of our national pastimes. When people move to a new house because they've "outgrown" their old house, what they likely mean is that their *junk* has outgrown their house. How many garages in America do you think are *not* used for car storage but for junk storage?

I want you to think about compulsive hoarding because it summarizes this chapter perfectly. Our physical spaces, filled with junk, mirror the spaces in our minds, hearts, and spirits, all filled with junk and disposable, worthless things. We are living in a mental and spiritual landfill. We are being buried alive in mental filth. Yet we love all these things and feel powerless to let go of any of them.

We do this because we are living the "good enough" kind of life that I described at the end of chapter 2. This is adult life, completely removed from our kindergarten selves. We have forgotten how to create. We live by our limitations, and we have settled for laziness and junk and ugliness. And our expectations are so low we don't think it can get any better than this.

This is what the epidemic of lost artists looks like: a world without beauty, hope, faith, or much else that God created us to experience.

Living in a mental landfill, of course, is a very unsatisfying way to live. It is not how we were *created* to live. Humans have endlessly pursued the divine because we want our lives to mean something besides the few decades we spend on Earth. We don't want to just leave behind a corpse and a houseful of junk that our kids will throw away. We want *permanence.*

We want a *legacy.*

What will you leave behind?

What are you creating with your life that is *timeless*? What will matter about your life when you are gone? Will your life have a positive impact that is worth remembering?

Creating something *timeless* will be a slow, meticulous process. It will not happen in a week or ten days. It will be more like an artist slowly chipping and smoothing a block of marble into a man. It will take time and patience and will be extraordinarily satisfying.

To live a "good" life, not just a "good enough" life, will require you to determine what your legacy is. Building your legacy will require turning back the clock and becoming that kindergartner you once were. It will require stripping off layers of old paint and dirt from your mind and regaining those lost childhood traits.

That's what we're going to do in the next three chapters.

QUESTIONS FOR THOUGHT

1. *What would I like my life to mean when it is over? What do I want my life to say about me?*

2. *What legacy am I building? What will I leave behind that will tell people about my life? Am I creating timeless things that will outlast me?*

3. *How much time and energy do I sacrifice by filling up my mental landfill?*

CHAPTER FOUR

COLORING inside the *LINES*

relearning how to create within the boundaries of life

4.1 Best Friends

Childhood friends are so important. We learn an incredible amount from our first best friend as children. They are our first nonfamily companion. We learn to laugh and play and argue and make up with friends. They provide a little training ground long before we meet our lifelong mates. Think for a moment about your best childhood friend.

I met mine in third grade.

I was a careful, quiet, and deliberate kid.

Brandon was . . . the opposite in every way.

He was rambunctious. He was energetic. He threw caution to the wind; or maybe he was just oblivious. I never figured out which. Sometimes, as we became teenagers and started dating girls, and began to think about our futures, even I could not understand our friendship. We just could not have been more *different.*

But we shared one thing in common as children. Brandon was an incredibly skilled artist. It was the one activity that he was diligent and thoughtful about. And he was a completely superior artist to me in every way.

But he never told me that.

Brandon and I shared many things in life. We spent our Boy Scout careers together. We would go to camp and bunk up together (not every year, because he was too messy).

Every once in a while, I lapsed in my cautiousness around him and we'd do something dumb together, like break open glow sticks and smear the glowing goop on ourselves. Prancing around in the dark with glowing hands, faces, and chests was fun—for about forty-three seconds, until it started burning our skin. Our much smarter friend had chosen not to participate, and when we started to panic, he casually told us, "Of course it's burning. That's cyalume and hydrogen peroxide. I would not put that on my skin if I were you."

I helped Brandon's family move into their new house. We walked across the stage together at high school graduation. We spent countless nights at each other's homes and watched countless terrible horror films together.

But before we could do all of that, our first outing together as third graders was to cut across his neighbors' yards and venture to the nearby creek. Every kid needs a secret getaway place. This was ours. Even though this muddy little ditch wound through neighborhoods and under cross streets, it felt like we had wandered far away from home, like pioneers.

But just as important for us as fellow artists, the creek was full of treasures. We would return with a sackful of rocks, carefully selected for the fossils they contained. Back at home, we would extract the fossils with tools and carefully replicate our discoveries with pencil and paper.

We weren't strictly scientists at the creek, though. Brandon also had an excellent stash of firecrackers, lighters, and other paraphernalia that he always brought to the creek, along with various action figures doomed to a brutal, firecracker-related demise. (Didn't everyone know one kid who always had a backpack full of contraband?) We knew the muddy, rocky creek bed was the least flammable and least supervised place for two ten-year-olds to play with fire and explosives. Safety first!

When we weren't at the creek, we were spread out all over the floor of one of our bedrooms, making artistic re-creations of all the various collector cards in our possession. Extensive collections of cards like *X-Men* were designed to steal the meager allowances of boys everywhere. But they also featured realistically rendered characters with dynamic poses and exaggerated musculature that provided endless artistic challenges. Between the fossils and the X-Men, we were almost like the old masters, like da Vinci and Michelangelo, studying nature, physics, and anatomy. Yep, we were a couple of third grade Renaissance men.

Brandon's tastes and talents always tended toward the bizarre and macabre, while mine tended toward the more fanciful. When a high school teacher found him filling an entire notebook page with sketches of gruesome shrunken heads, she reported him to the counselor's office. It was a good thing that the counselor was a longtime friend of his family, or Brandon may have been sent off to psychotherapy, and the world would be deprived of his gifts. Today he is an excellent tattoo artist and spends his days permanently inking bizarre and macabre images on human skin.

4.2 The Perfect Role Model

Like many people, I learned a great deal from the friends I spent time with as a child. But it would be difficult to overstate the impact that some family members had on me.

I think I learned how to be a perfectionist from my maternal grandfather.

The man was an engineer for a large corporation. He was mostly deaf, not just in his hearing but with most social courtesies. And he was a large man, quite tall, with a big voice, which he could use to be extremely harsh, critical, and belligerent. When I played checkers against him as a boy, he played for blood sport. He took no five-year-old prisoners.

My mother told us about how as a child, she would bring home report cards, full of As.

"This is a 93 percent," Grandpa would say to Mom.

"Sure is!" she'd beam.

"What happened to the other 7 percent?" he'd ask.

And so it was that my mother and her two sisters labored under a father for whom even perfection wasn't perfect enough. He was the kind of man whose daughters would grow up and call him "Wally" instead of "Dad."

Throughout the house were signs of Grandpa's home improvement activities—the extra little room he had built or the garden boxes outside. So much of the house had his little touches. My mother told us about how he seeded their yard by laying out a grid of string and placing little sprigs of grass, evenly spaced across the yard, by hand. She told us how he had calculated precise measurements of fertilizer to dispense on the new grass. Of course, such a meticulously engineered yard required being mowed not once but *twice*, lest an errant blade of grass escape the first pass of the blade. Her job was to fetch his beer, which afforded her the chance to drink out of the can defiantly before delivering it to him.

My mother never decorated a Christmas tree when she was a kid. It wasn't that her dad didn't believe in Christmas. He just didn't trust kids with the heady task of hanging ornaments. He had drawn up a diagram of where each Christmas ornament should be located on the tree, and he felt more at ease ensuring himself that everything was in place for maximum yuletide cheer.

Of course, even the act of opening presents was an ordeal, as he refused to *rip* the wrapping paper, preferring instead to try the patience of children, adults, and probably even baby Jesus every year.

Every once in a while, Grandpa would have a little woodworking project for my brother and me to do with him. Most of the time, these projects were an exercise less in craftsmanship and more in patience for us (much like watching him open Christmas presents). We were his only grandsons, and the duties of learning Grandpa's craft fell on our shoulders. Grandpa was a meticulous man. He was a perfectionist of all perfection.

By the time I knew him, Grandpa's big hobby was his miniature train set. "Miniature" is a loose term, because although the trains themselves were miniatures, the set itself was quite massive. It filled a large basement room. It was about thirty feet long, and ten feet wide. It was a colossal work of great mathematical genius . . . and having too much time on one's retired hands. Great mountains and lakes were sculpted out of plaster. Tracks circled the landscape. Little German houses were scattered around. The entire thing was propped up on a custom built platform about four feet off the floor. Underneath was an unbelievable array of wires. The control panel housed a dizzying number of switches. On the wall, three charts showed a scale drawing of the tracks with little lights that could be flipped on or off, indicating whether the intersections of the track were "open" or "closed."

One Thanksgiving, we went down to the basement to see the trains. Grandpa brought us to his workshop to show us something new. He gave us a piece of clear wire and told us to hold one end up to a lit flashlight. The opposite end of the wire lit up.

"It's called 'fiberoptic' cable," he told us.

Grandpa was wiring every house and streetlight with fiberoptic cable, years before it was being used to deliver high-speed Internet to homes. There were even tiny traffic signals. When we turned off the overhead lights, the entire town glowed like a modern city. It was miraculous and magical, and I assumed that all boys had a massive train set to play with on Thanksgiving.

When Grandpa died, my brother and I got the trains. He had

done us the courtesy of boxing them up for us. Every train, every house, every little prop was in its original box. Every strand of wire was bundled and labeled. Even boxed up without the platform and mountains, the collection took up an enormous space. Grandpa never threw away a scrap of an instruction manual or a piece of packaging. Everything was in gleaming mint condition. Grandpa had purchased the very best for himself. It was a magnificent treasure trove of German-made, Marklin brand trains and accessories. We could have reassembled the entire set, exactly as Grandpa had left it, wire for wire, and nothing would have made him prouder.

He would've killed us if he knew how much we got for his trains on eBay.

On one Thanksgiving visit, my mother showed me something interesting. Adjacent to the magnificent train room was a room filled with junk. It appeared to have been, at one time, a party room. It was spacious, and along the wall was a rather handsome kitchenette, complete with cabinets, a sink, dishwasher, and refrigerator. It would be the perfect place to make drinks for guests. Mom told me that Grandpa had built the room. I was impressed. But why was the room filled with junk? It looked as if it had not entertained people for a long time.

"Look at this," my mother said, almost with a sparkle in her eye.

She pulled on one of the cabinet knobs. A beam hung along the ceiling, parallel to the cabinets. The cabinet door opened *almost* ninety degrees before hitting the beam and stopping with a thud.

That *thud* was why the room was filled with junk and not used for entertaining people. Grandpa had made a mistake— a stupid, amateur mistake. He had not correctly calculated the clearance needed for the cabinet doors to miss the beam. The entire room was assembled, and then the cabinets would not open all the way. If the doors had just been a half-inch narrower, they would have cleared the beam, and the cabinets and the room would be perfect.

This was my grandfather's work. This meticulous, driven, perfectionist of a man had made something *imperfect.* And the room that he must have spent so much time to build was used for storage.

I imagined the frustration Grandpa felt. After all that effort and time, he came up short. He was *not* perfect. It was a feeling I would become acquainted with as a newly married man, attempting to furnish our new apartment. Every piece of furniture from Target would need assembling, and every assembly would be marked by a leg or a door or some other piece attached incorrectly. And then those screws that aren't supposed to come back out would have to be pried back out, and I'd start again. Yes, I have serious limitations as a carpenter.

I concluded chapter 2 by asking you if you are living a "good" life or a "good enough" life. In chapter 3, we explored the ramifications of a society settling for "good enough."

Remember the three phases of evolution that happened to each of us as we grew up? First, creating stopped being important, as other priorities took over. Second, we became self-aware and discovered our limitations. Finally, after we discovered our limitations, we became defeated, or just lazy. We stopped being generous with our creating. Since then, you and I have spent much of our adult lives living on the "good enough" plan.

In this chapter, we're going to start undoing those phases. We'll start with the final phase and work backward. The final phase was the one where we became defeated by our own limitations and got lazy.

It is time to stop living for "good enough."

4.3 Following Directions and Nonconformity

"Why do we have to listen to you, Mr. Appling? Aren't we *just* painting?"

Even a third grader, with a comment like that one, can really get under my skin. It is difficult to describe how it feels to have a well-planned lesson ready to go, to be excited for the hour ahead, and then be thrown off your game by a third grade heckler and his smart-aleck questions.

First, *no* we weren't *just* painting. I intended to teach a new technique.

Second, the inherent disrespect of the question indicated I had nothing to say that was worth a child's time.

And third, kids who hate following directions are going to have a hard time in life.

"You're right," I said, putting down my brush. "That's exactly what I was just about to tell you to do. Your instructions are 'just paint.'"

I guess I woke up on the sarcastic side of the bed that day.

"Really?" a few kids asked, while others scrunched their noses.

"No, not really," I answered, smirking. "See how ridiculous that sounds? Now pick up your brushes and follow along with me. We are learning a new technique today."

I wonder if Jesus was ever sassed by a nine-year-old.

I give lots of directions in class. And that third grader was hardly the first to ignore me. Some kids cannot seem to believe that I am there to help them. I am usually giving directions about how to do a project correctly, or how to use supplies, or I am just trying to keep the room from devolving into a chaotic *Lord of the Flies* situation.

"Is that how you'd used a hairbrush? You bang it on your head until your hair looks right?" I have just caught a kid mashing his paintbrush into his paper, destroying the bristles. It's called a "brush" for a reason, kids. You *brush* with it. If you treat a brush like a hammer, pretty soon you do not have a brush—or a painting.

I never understood the obsessive levels of control schoolteachers keep over their kids until I became a teacher. The amount of chaos and noise that is possible when a room of children is out of control is unreal.

But it is not just about keeping control when I give directions.

I am attempting to teach my students something about the world. Because the only alternative to following directions is the ever-popular *nonconformity*.

And nonconformity, it turns out, is not all it's cracked up to be.

Nonconformity is all the rage. So many people want to be unique. They want to buck the trend. They want to color outside the lines, if you will. Being a "conformist" is thought to be a terrible thing. People who conform are thought to be easily manipulated and controlled by governments and evil religious organizations.

The popular belief is that what's more important than conforming is "expressing yourself." It sounds a lot like those kindergartners' mothers saying, "Just be creative!"

If someone wants to dress differently or try to be a nonconformist, fine by me. We need some people to be trendsetters in the world. But even if you believe yourself to be a nonconformist, there are all kinds of activities that are best done while following directions.

A cake turns out best when a recipe is followed. If you want to be a nonconformist in the kitchen, like me, it is best to stay away from baking and do something else. My wife is very much the recipe follower, which is good when exact measurements are needed, such as in baking. I suspect her attention to detail is part of what makes her an effective veterinarian.

I, on the other hand, learned from my dad to scrounge the pantry and throw random things together, which is better for casseroles. You also wouldn't want me poking around inside your dog.

When we are doing a math problem, or learning to drive, or baking a cake, it is best if we follow directions. It is not necessary for us to start from scratch, to make our *own* mistakes in a trial and error process in an effort to make a chocolate cake. Betty Crocker has already gone to the trouble of trial and error. When baking a cake, as in many situations, insisting on making your own mistakes, being a nonconformist is a real waste of time.

Most of us think that learning from your own experience is the highest form of learning, and that usually means making your own mistakes. Next time you're inclined to think that, just tell a toddler to go ahead and touch that hot stove so he can have a "learning experience."

4.4 A Life Full of Constraints

Directions from an instruction manual or from a teacher represent *constraints*. They are meant to keep us on the correct path. They are meant for our benefit and convenience.

As humans, we are also subject to all kinds of natural constraints.

Our natural bodies are compelled to sleep for approximately one-third of our lives. We are compelled to eat a few times a day. We are constrained by finances, like it or not. We are constrained by our health, our talents, our shortcomings, and ultimately by our mortality.

To a nonconformist, all these constraints must seem appalling.

As humans, we are constantly running into constraints. Our first constraints were artificial ones, placed on us by our parents. *Don't touch that. Stop right there.* As we grew up, it slowly dawned on us that there were things at which we were untalented. At some other time, it dawned on us that our parents were limited in their abilities too.

I suspect that when it comes to dealing with these human constraints, there are two kinds of people. There are the people who give up. They get lazy. They stop trying and adopt a fatalistic, "good enough" lifestyle. They live life by their limitations. They settle for an unsatisfactory existence, however you define that.

And there are the other people, who are always trying to push against the constraints of life.

Ever since God first said, "Don't do that," and Adam and Eve did it anyway, people have insisted on making their own mistakes, trying to be nonconformists. As third graders, we didn't like listening to teachers. When we were teenagers, our parents' IQ dropped by about fifty points, so we stopped listening to them. As adults, we dream of winning the lottery, or we just rack up a lot of credit card debt. Or we try to defy genetics or the aging process. Or we push against the constraints of marital fidelity.

We still entertain dreams of a life without constraints.

Trying to rebel against the constraints in your life, trying to color outside the lines that have been laid out for you, is not a recipe for success. You will not live a "good" life or leave behind a good legacy. It is a recipe for frustration, for discontentment, for defeat in life. You will never defy the ultimate realities that constrain all of us.

Nor is resigning in defeat the way to go through life. There is no point in being depressed, in wasting your life because you are not as talented or beautiful or rich as you would like. You will certainly not live a good life by constantly thinking about your life in terms of your limitations.

I should know. When I was a child, my parents told me I could do anything I wanted to do. My father thought I was brilliant. I could be president if I wanted. But growing up was a process of discovering this was not the case. I was not as brilliant as I had assumed. I probably could not be president. And with each new discovery of my limitations in life, I have struggled with the accompanying discontentment, anxiety, depression, and frustrated ambition.

I had a choice to make. Do I attempt to rebel against the constraints of my life? Do I try to deny they exist? Do I resign my fate and give up trying?

No. There must be a better option.

 CREATIVE GIANTS Ole Kirk Christiansen

OLE KIRK CHRISTIANSEN (1891–1958):

Ole Kirk Christiansen was a carpenter from Denmark whose name is virtually unknown today. Yet his work still brings joy and fosters creativity among millions of children today. The company he built produces Lego bricks.

The word *lego* means "play well," and his invention has been inspiring children for decades to do just that. The toys are unique because they allow children an amazing level of creative freedom. Yet that creative freedom is possible because of a perfect balance of constraints. Lego bricks can only interlock top-to-bottom, thanks to the signature little nubs on the top of each brick. Yet this restraint allows nearly infinite combinations, with greater freedom than toys such as Lincoln Logs or Erector Sets. Lego bricks produced today are still compatible with the bricks produced over fifty years ago at their inception.

4.5 Beauty through Constraints

When God formed the universe, He set limits on the sea to separate it from the land. He set the atmosphere around the Earth to separate it from space.

And He created life. He made plants to be immobile, rooted to the ground. He made elephants with trunks but no hands. He made fish to swim but not to walk. He made cheetahs to run fast, but He gave them small hearts, so they can only run short distances.

When God formed Adam from the dust, He didn't make him the strongest or fastest animal. He made Adam rather delicate, with skin that needed shade from the sun and feet that needed protection from the ground. He made Adam to need to eat and sleep and follow all kinds of routines born of the limitations of his body and mind. And God told Adam and Eve that one day they would return to the dust.

God created a world restrained by gravity, constrained by innumerable physical laws. He created animal and plant life, each kind with its own strengths and limitations. And He created humanity to live and die by all kinds of constraints.

God created all of these constraints and limitations—and called them *good*.

That's the lesson we didn't learn as third graders. Or we forgot it and we've been paying the price ever since.

Whenever mothers tell their children to just "be creative," or children whine because I have only given them three colors of paint, they are missing a very important reality about the necessity, nay the *beauty* of constraints.

What would the universe look like without any constraints placed on it? Chaos.

The same is true of a piece of child's art with absolutely no constraints. It is absolute chaos. Without the constraints of discipline, a child is wildly directionless and ultimately unhappy. Without the constraints of commonly shared morality, society falls into chaos.

It is the lines and constraints that make the universe orderly, society livable, children mature, and art beautiful. We call the constraints *design*. The artist decides if he will create a representational or an abstract painting. That's a constraint. He decides the style and the media he will use. That's another constraint. Then he decides the subject matter, and the constraints go on and on and the design becomes more defined. If he desires to paint a tree, there are some essential limitations he will have to abide by in order to make his tree a tree. If he goes outside of those constraints, his tree will no longer be a tree but something else. The Sistine Chapel isn't great because it's both abstract *and* representational. It is amazing because it is a pinnacle in a very *specific*, *limited*, *defined* kind of art. The chapel is not supposed to be a modern piece of abstract art. If it was, it would be a failure.

A piece of children's art becomes beautiful and refined when a child is taught to work within constraints, to create some lines, some boundaries, *and color inside them*, to know when a piece of art is *finished*.

All the "good" constraints God placed on the universe (which we call "laws of nature") create all the beauty we are privy to in God's creation. When God was creating the universe, He didn't draw a line and call it "gravity" and then say, "Dang, where's My eraser?" because He really wanted to see what a planet would look like without gravity (or because He just wanted to see all His little people humorously fly off the planet). He preferred to draw lines in ink. When God drew a line in the sand and made a promise, or said, "I will do this," or "I will never do that," He didn't go back and color outside the lines He had drawn.

What if the very constraints on your life, which defeat and frustrate you, which you try to rebel against to no avail, have been placed on your life *because they are good*? What if the constraints on your life were there to actually make your life *beautiful*? What if you learned that even the mistakes that have marked your life can be redeemed? What if you learned, rather than to be defeated by the lines that have been marked on your life, to *color inside the lines*?

The most beautiful marriages are colored within the lines of fidelity and commitment. Being a good parent means coloring vigorously within the lines of parental duty. Becoming a good leader, employee, craftsman, or anything else requires that you master coloring within some very specific lines that define the job.

But the human folly is to always try to erase lines and constraints that have been drawn. God tells us to color inside the lines; that our lives will be better if we stay inside the lines He has drawn. We instead scribble around and always with consequences. Our lives turn out a little less beautiful.

Children and adults react to constraints in different ways and with different effects.

Some children try to constantly push against the constraints a teacher or parents put on them. Many adults do the same thing, dreaming of a life without any limitations. Other children and adults are defeated by constraints and limitations. They adopt a fatalistic attitude that life is hopeless and meaningless. They settle for laziness and their lives remain unfulfilled.

And then there are the children and adults who are able to discern the good, *positive* boundaries that God has placed on their lives, and the negative, unnecessary boundaries they place on themselves. They learn to let go of the self-defeating pursuit of trying to erase the lines in their lives, or pretend they are not there, or that they do not matter. It means realizing that inside your lines—the lines of money, talent, time, energy, health, job, beauty, disability, and every other line that you see as a limit—there is still a lot of room for vibrant, joyful color.

People prove this every day. They defy the odds. They do amazing things despite some limitation or awful circumstance. They become famous and people see them on the news and read the book and watch the movie about their lives because they are amazing.

You know these people:

The woman who escapes exploitation and then helps other women.

The child who achieves victory despite a disability.

The man who overcomes years of abuse and rewrites his future.

Of course, you and I also know the *other kind* of person, the kind of person who is defeated by lines, the person who *never* changes his life, who stays hopeless, who just makes excuses. This is the kind of person who wants encouragement, maybe even pity, but never invests those things into real change. The only thing he creates is excuses.

CREATIVE GIANTS Theodor Geisel

THEODOR GEISEL (1904–1991): Theodor Geisel made a career as a humorist and political cartoonist. But everyone knows him as Dr. Seuss. Geisel found the state of education in America deplorable, specifically the literature that was used to teach children to read. He found children's literature impossibly boring. Why would any child bother to learn to read when the books offered no incentive?

Geisel had been writing children's books and doing advertising, but his career took a turn when he was issued a challenge by a chairman of textbook publisher Houghton Mifflin. The challenge was steep with limitations and constraints. Houghton Mifflin had a list of words, around three hundred words, which first graders should know how to read. Geisel's challenge was

to write a book using 250 of the prescribed words, and no others.

Several months later, Geisel published what critics called his tour de force: *The Cat in the Hat*. It wasn't that coloring inside the lines, so to speak, was easy for Geisel. It was one of the steepest and most frustrating challenges to date for a man used to making up words when he needed to make a rhyme. He even completed half of a book about a king cat and a queen cat before he realized that "queen" was not on the list of prescribed words.

In the end, *The Cat in the Hat* clocked in with 223 of the required words, and a mere thirteen extra words not from the list. Not to mention the book keeps strict triple meter rhyme, and has been enthralling children with the pleasures of reading for decades since its publication.[4]

Creating excuses is always easier than creating change.

There have been times in my life when I have fallen into a slump of excuses and apathy, and the result is always the same. If you are in the habit of creating excuses, nurturing a victimhood mentality, and just generally being lazy because you think your life is unfair, please be careful. People may encourage you. They may tell you that things will get better, that you are smart and capable. But people, even the encouraging ones, like to think they are making a difference. You are unlikely to find many people who will encourage you, despite all your determination, to *not* change. If they can see that their encouragement is having no effect on you, they are more likely than not to give up altogether, and then you will have no pity, no encouragement, and still no change in your life. You will just have those same lines and boundaries, but no color.

4.6 Perfection

Every morning I get up a little bit before 6:00 A.M. Some days, I'm disciplined enough to go for a jog. I dress in a button-down shirt. I'll be out the door before my wife wakes up to go to her job. During this quiet time, my mind plays through the day ahead, and one phrase repeats in my head.

Being a teacher is a bit of a lonely profession. We work with other adults, but that just means we work *near* other adults. Our rooms are our domain, but the nearest adult is next door. It is just us, faced with a classroom of children. We are truly an army of one. I greet other teachers in the hallway each morning on my way to my room, and one phrase repeats in my head.

Being an art teacher in particular is a strange paradox. For the first hour, I prepare. I am very analytically minded, which I know is unusual for an art teacher, but I don't know how I would get anything done if I was not so analytical. At 7:30 in the morning, the room is quiet and serene. I leave half the lights off as I feed the little red betta fish, a gift from a trio of fourth grade girls. I do some cleaning, reorganize materials, hang up new artwork, look over my notes for high school art history. I keep a journal of the lessons we do and make notes on where I went wrong as a teacher.

Before becoming a teacher, I visited my mother's second grade classroom and smirked at how much control teachers exercised over students. So much energy seemed to be wasted, in my opinion, on lining up quietly or using the bathroom at the proper time. Now I pore over seating charts for my own classroom with the strategy of a chess master. Which students should sit next to one another? Which students could help one another? Which students are toxic together? How do I keep those two students as far apart as possible? There are a million combinations and considerations to make.

I create demonstrations of the projects the students will do. Every project, for every grade level, I work through ahead of time, dozens of art projects every year. It allows me to see how kids should be instructed, and what pitfalls they may encounter. It gives them a visual reference to know what their goal is. And it never hurts for the teacher to be able to show work that impresses kids. I feel bad for math teachers who have to try to impress kids by solving quadratic equations. No one likes quadratic equations. During this first quiet hour of the day, one phrase repeats in my head.

The other side of the art teacher's world is an all-out assault on the senses. "Bombardment" is the word that comes to mind. An hour at a time, kids are jostling for attention, instruction, or validation. There are messes to manage. There are problems to solve constantly. I am a teacher, a trainer, a janitor, a counselor, and a drill sergeant. It's just me against the forces of anarchy. And in the midst of the commotion, one phrase repeats in my head.

Finally, the day is done, and I drive home, weary and tired. My mental camcorder plays through the day's conversations and confrontations. I am happy with some interactions I had, and I mentally replay those scenes a couple of times. Others I wish I could erase and rewrite. I think about students who are struggling and need special encouragement next time. On the way home, the same phrase repeats in my head that has been on a loop all day.

The phrase is a simple prayer.

God, please make me a better teacher than I was yesterday.

I desperately want God to answer that prayer. I want to be more compassionate, more motivating, more knowledgeable, more disciplined, more *everything*.

I want to be *better* because I start thinking about this perceived need we humans have, to push against lines and create excuses, and I think about the last constraint placed on us, the last line that we will have to learn to color inside if we are ever going to leave anything behind worth looking at:

Perfection.

As humans, our lines are clearly drawn, and perfection is not inside the lines. If you are wishing for perfection in any pursuit, your life will end unfulfilled.

I see myself in the perfectionist students. They are struggling and frustrated and erasing marks on their paper that won't go away. I quietly whisper, "Finished is better than perfect." If they continue to focus on perfection at the expense of all else, they will achieve nothing.

I've slowly learned to let go of perfectionism. You can get a perfect score on a science project, but who can say if a painting is perfect? There certainly are no 100 percents awarded in life. I cannot pray to be a *perfect* teacher. I cannot even pray to have one *perfect* day as an art teacher. I've learned simply to pray that God would help be to be *better* than the day before.

Even my grandfather, who pursued perfection in all that he created, built some lousy cabinets. It appeared that he gave up in frustration and filled the room with junk to cover his mistake.

As artists and as humans, we have to learn to color inside the line that is imperfect, messy, or even a *mistake*. Nothing in your life will ever be just right. There will always be pressures and conflicts, making errant smudges and splatters on your life. Living a "good" life is not about living a "perfect" life.

An amateur artist tries to erase a mistake. A master artist learns how to work with a mistake.

QUESTIONS FOR THOUGHT

1. *What limitations are routinely placed on my life? Do I feel I don't have enough time, money, the right personality, etc.?*

2. How do I allow those limitations to dictate my life and level of happiness and satisfaction? In other words, how do I allow those limitations to cause me to settle for a "good enough" life?

3. Which of the "lines" or limitations in my life are permanent? Which can realistically be erased or moved?

4. How can I live within my limitations and still achieve something good with my life? How can I learn to be content and satisfied with the circumstances I have?

CHAPTER FIVE

Freedom to *FAIL*

relearning how to take necessary risks

5.1 **What Girls Want**

In high school, I discovered there was one commodity I desired above all else: the attention of girls. And I learned that to get girls, a guy has to have a skill. Girls only want boyfriends who have great skills. And since I did not have nunchaku skills or bow hunting skills or computer hacking skills, there was really only one skill I could use to compete for female attention: art.

Over the course of high school, I carefully developed this little shtick of giving paintings to girls. Cheap canvas, no frame, just the best painting of a happy sunset or some trees that a high school girl could get. I even wrapped up the paintings in brown grocery bag paper and twine, just to lend an element of surprise. Once I gave one away, it was easy. Other girls heard that some less-deserving classmate had one of my paintings in her bedroom, and they were *asking* me, twirling their hair in their fingers, if I could do a painting for them.

I chuckled to myself and almost felt sorry for those poor hapless meatheads on the football team. What did they have to garner female admiration? *Did you see that touchdown I scored? I did that for you, babe.* They had nothing . . . except for giant muscles . . . and chiseled jaws.

I gave paintings to girls I had no intention of dating and girls I fully intended to date, because I believed what Dad said: girls talk. The racket earned me a few dates. I was still no ladykiller. But I bet after the publication of this book those girls will be glad they kept those paintings (if they did), because by now, they have probably appreciated into the tens of dollars, counting the value of the canvas.

I heard that one of my equally unathletic friends was secretly writing songs and serenading girls to attract attention. I don't know, singing to girls sounds kind of pathetic to me. Slipping paintings into girls' car windows is way cooler.

5.2 Failure Is Fun

My brother and I lived next door to two boys our age. We played with the neighbor boys all the time. We played baseball and had secret club meetings. Since this was in the early nineties, the neighbor boys possessed one very intriguing piece of technology my brother and I had never played with: a Nintendo Entertainment System.

Of course I had seen the commercials, but I did not understand the appeal until I witnessed it in person. There was Super Mario, in all his pixelated glory. The sky was blue and there was a cheerful tune humming through the TV. I grabbed the controller and Mario started to move to the right. With the press of a button, he avoided a grumbly looking, slow-moving passerby, hopped a couple more times . . . and fell directly into a bottomless pit. The game played a lighthearted tune to indicate its disapproval, and I was docked a turn.

I was hooked.

It did not matter how many times our mustachioed hero fell down a hole, or bumped into a passing turtle, and I had to hear that same tune of dissatisfaction from the game, I gladly, joyfully persisted. I was a terrible player. Gaining skill and coordination would be a long process of trial and error. I didn't care.

Super Mario Brothers single-handedly rescued an industry that was about to collapse. And the console it was sold on was a pretty remarkable little gray box. *Super Mario Brothers* was even packed with *Duck Hunt* and an orange gun to shoot at the TV. It was brilliant in its simplicity.

After a couple of months of playing at the neighbors, my brother and I decided we'd save up and pool our money for our own gaming console. Playing games became a family gathering with my brother and mother. Not Dad, though. His job was to make sure we were not playing too much.

On some Saturday mornings, the three of us would take a turn or two at a game. Mom would be playing while Dad left for the day, saying, "Dear, you should probably let the boys have a turn at it." We'd then go outside or do chores for the rest of the

CREATIVE GIANTS Shigeru Miyamoto

SHIGERU MIYAMOTO (1952–): Shigeru Miyamoto is one of the most revered creative visionaries of modern history to those who know his name. While his name might not be recognizable or even pronounceable to many Westerners, he's treated like a rock star in Japan. Regardless, nearly everyone recognizes his creations.

Miyamoto became the central visionary designer at Nintendo in Kyoto, Japan. As a young man, he created the industry's most recognizable and loved mascots and games, including *Super Mario Brothers*.

So why is Mario a plumber in overalls? It turns out, Mario's iconic design is all about coloring inside some very restrictive lines, or pixels, as it were. When Miyamoto designed Mario for his first appearance in *Donkey Kong*, the power of arcade machines was extremely limited. Every pixel and animation cost processing power. Mario himself was rather diminutive on-screen.

Miyamoto decided that a red shirt and blue overalls would distinguish Mario's arms from his body. A mustache would help shape his face. And why does he wear a red cap? Because the few pixels used to draw a cap was more economical than drawing and animating hair.[5]

Thus, the iconic face of video games was born of the extreme technological constraints on his creator.

Brilliance in simplicity, born of constraints. As with Jim Henson and Edwin Binney, Miyamoto (and anyone who has ever touched a computer) owes a debt to an unfortunately less famous female. GRACE HOPPER (1906–1992) was a U.S. Navy officer and a brilliant pioneering computer scientist. Her vision to bring computers to a much wider audience than just military applications led to some of the most fundamental advancements in making computers friendly to programmers and users, not just mathematicians.

day and eight hours later, we'd reconvene for another round of games. And wouldn't you know it, just as Mom was starting to play, Dad would return from his errands. She was caught red-handed. She had been playing eight hours and hadn't let her own sons have a turn! Those were the only times Dad encouraged us to play *more*, just to get the controller away from Mom.

5.3 A Grand Contradiction

The focus of the previous chapter was making a resolution to embrace the messy and imperfect in your life, to not live life *stuck* inside your limitations and restraints but to *embrace* those limitations and just get coloring. After all, they aren't going anywhere.

In order to do that, we are going to have to scrape another layer of old paint from our minds. We are going to have to get a little closer to our five-year-old selves. Deeper in our past is the point in time when we stopped being generous with our creativity, and instead began to focus on comparing ourselves with our peers.

We became afraid to fail.

In the early 90s, gaming was still the obsession of young boys, but more and more people today, men and women of all ages, are discovering the joy of gaming through social media or smart phones. I bring this up to illustrate a grand contradiction in our modern world.

I love to see students striving to do their best. I love to see students trying to do "good" work and not just "good enough" work. What is not so great is seeing kids paralyzed by a fear of failure. They are in the grip of realizing their limitations, and they are becoming deathly afraid of them on their way to giving up altogether. *What will people think of me if I try and fail?* they think to themselves. They are no longer being generous with their work as the kindergartners are. They are beginning to be ashamed of their work.

They cannot put a mark on the paper without worrying that it might not be "correct." They are constantly asking for my approval; or worse, they'll just sit and stare at the blank paper and endure my prodding and encouragement as if I am torturing them. They'll tell me they don't like their work. They want to start over. I ask them if they are an art critic or an art teacher. "No," they say. "Then leave the criticizing to me and just keep at it."

Some art projects are just tougher than others.

Sometimes, that is my fault. I choose the wrong project. I overestimate the students' abilities, or I just don't explain it very well. Other times kids just give up. Still, I see every failed project (whether it's my fault or theirs) as a learning opportunity.

At the end of one particularly tough project, a lot of kids were not exactly pleased with their work. I had pushed their skills to their very limits.

"How many professional artists do you think are happy with every piece of art they ever made?" I ask.

Most kids assume that an artist at the professional level must be so great that every painting is a masterpiece. It's just not true. Artists reuse canvases all the time, covering up a painting they were dissatisfied with. Experts can now detect these failed paintings with powerful X-rays. A Van Gogh painting of some flowers was discovered to be covering a painting from several years before of two boxers locked in battle.

Assuming that professional artists love everything they do is like assuming that a professional basketball player makes every shot, or a doctor never makes a mistake, or a writer doesn't need an editor.

There are two facts of life that kids miss: that professional "experts" still make mistakes, still fail, and that professionals are often their own toughest critics.

Somewhere along the way children learn that failure is something to be feared, rather than to be learned from and embraced. Modern adults developed a strange notion sometime ago that failure must hurt kids' self-esteem. So efforts were made to manufacture an artificial world for children to live in, free of all forms of competition and the possibility of failure. They told kids that they were all special and equally good, and no one was a loser (because losing was no longer possible).

Children are easily manipulated, so they believed this. Consequently, they become afraid to fail. Failure became an "unknown," and the unknown is almost always frightening.

Contrast this artificial reality (where failure does not exist or is avoided at all costs) to the other artificial reality of games, beloved by so many. Children (and adults) fail *dozens* of times every day. They do it gladly, even joyfully. They keep failing and trying again through the pervasive world of games. When I failed to move Mario past the bottomless pit, there was no mistaking it. I had failed. My number of chances was docked by one, and the familiar "fail" tune played. No hand-holding or sugarcoating or "participation" ribbon to soften the blow. Parents and teachers may feel compelled to award a few points for effort. But the cold, heartless gray box by the TV told me the truth in no uncertain terms. I failed, and if I failed enough, the game would be over.

Completing the game would require that I learn not to fail. And millions of children around the world learned right along with me, ever so tediously, how to move our pixelated friend to the final stage. Success only came with hard work. I still love relearning this lesson with games against friends. And children still learn this lesson every day in front of the TV, before being driven to their noncompetitive peewee soccer leagues.

It does seem ironic that the artificial world of games provides a more realistic scenario of reality than the artificial world that failure-averse parents try to create. As we grow older, we realize our limitations and our stomach for failure seems to shrink. Our risk tolerance for failure is lowered until we become adults and believe that failure hurts everyone's self-esteem.

5.4 Time to Start Failing

Maybe like me, your fear of failure has often been a paralyzing condition. Your life is stuck somewhere you don't really want to be. You aren't sinking, but you aren't really *moving* either. You know your limitations and you feel too paralyzed by the risk of failure, so you never step out and try anything new. You learned that failure was intolerable long ago and your ego just cannot handle it.

But without the risk of failure, where would the world be?

Right where you are: afraid, and stuck. If everyone were afraid of failure, then Nikola Tesla would have given up his research that launched the modern electrical age, no boy would ever get a date to a school dance, and no games would ever be played.

For me, junior high P.E. was the most public display of failure in my entire life.

There I was, the scrawny kid with the glasses, in my dorky little gym shorts. My name was written in permanent marker on my shirt, in case anyone forgot who I was.

It was basketball season. Coach divided us up into teams. He only addressed us by last names. Rather than adding an air of formality, this seemed more dehumanizing. The game was a simple shooting relay. Line up, shoot the ball, keep shooting until you make a basket. Then pass to the next player in line.

And, of course, my last name starts with "A," so I was always up first. I quietly shook my fist at the heavens for my last name.

The whistle blew. I took a shot. And missed. Another shot—miss.

I had exactly three moments of athletic glory in my childhood. When I was eight, I kicked the winning point during kick ball. In high school, I made a couple of great catches in the outfield on the rotational baseball team my friends and I set up.

That day in the gym was not one of my moments of glory.

"You suck, Appling!"

Ouch. My classmates' comments were a bit more wounding than the playful tune that played when Mario fell in a pit.

Finally I finished. My teammates reiterated: I suck.

To an unathletic kid like me, P.E. was the biggest crock on

the planet. My limitations were on display for everyone to see. I failed on a daily basis.

I learned an interesting defensive tactic to salvage my pride. I told people I wasn't even trying, that I didn't care, that P.E. was not worth my effort. If I didn't sink a basket or make a goal or score a point, it was because I did not deem the task worthy of expending any effort.

In fact, I *was* trying. I was trying *desperately* not to fail. Failing was hard. I spent almost as much energy trying to sink a basket as I did trying to appear as if I was *not* actually trying to sink a basket.

It is really too bad that junior high P.E. was so often an environment where failure was not a safe option. My failure to shoot the basketball accurately stuck with me for years afterward. It took a lot of courage for me to join a gym as a young adult, because it seemed to me that gyms were not for scrawny people like me. They were for people who did not *need* to go to the gym. Gyms were places where good-looking people paid to be good-looking in public.

And when I joined a gym, the same fear remained implanted in my mind from long ago.

"Errrrrrrghhhhhaaaaahhhh!"

Some guy was making loud guttural sounds next to the mirrors while he lifted weights. A gym is the one and only public place, except a restroom, where such noises are socially acceptable, apparently. I knew that if I tried to make impressive guttural noises while weight lifting, it would sound dumb. I hadn't practiced making guttural sounds at home, and introverts like me feel the need to rehearse such things privately. So I sucked in my breath and lifted silently.

Over on the other side of the room was the hoop and the rack of basketballs beckoning me.

Should I pick one up?

What was my limitation? Lack of skill and practice.

What was the perceived consequence of failure? Embarrassment.

Result: I stayed inside my limitation and did not pick up a basketball.

How silly is that? It is extraordinarily silly. Chances are very good that none of the old men at the gym would've harassed me had I started throwing air balls all over the place—unless I hit one of them in his artificial hip with an errant shot.

Fear of failure looms over everyone in some way. Somewhere in your life, you are holding back, hiding yourself from others, despite what you *want* to do. You want to do something fun. You want to share with others. You want to be generous with yourself. But you perceive the consequences of failure to be too great. So you become a self-fulfilling prophecy and never try.

Students are shocked to learn that even professional artists *do not* like every piece of art they produce. In fact, most artists are their own toughest critics. Fear binds adults throughout their lives, too, preventing them from ever accomplishing anything. We have to be free of the fear that we will stumble and make something that is not great. Just like every writer tries again and again to get the right words (Mark Twain struggled for eleven years to complete *The Adventures of Huckleberry Finn*), and the best basketball players miss more shots than they make. Heck, the best baseball players miss an average of *seven* pitches for every *three* they hit. It is only adults who accept that most of what they do will *not* be great who end up making *some* great things to share with the world, as they were meant to do.

Take Abraham Lincoln, an abject failure in business and life. He was struck with tragedy and bad luck and mental illness. His first love interest died and his second one rejected him before he finally met his wife-to-be. His exploits in life continually blew up in his face. His private life was fraught with failure and depression. He would have been completely forgotten if he had been afraid to make a mark on the world. Yet Americans only remember him for his success, only possible because he never retreated after failure.

Contrast Lincoln to J. D. Salinger, one of the twentieth century's most celebrated authors. *Catcher in the Rye* was a critical and commercial success. But Salinger himself was a harsh self-critic and was petrified of failure and critique from others. He lived as a recluse, wrote privately in a cabin, and never again allowed anyone to read his creations. He deprived the world of what may have been works of genius. And for what? The possible embarrassment of a bad book.

And he did not even have to contend with one-star reviews on Amazon.

Remember that everything that is created will have a critic. That is why being generous with what we create is risky business. Every painting will invite someone to wish that the artist had painted something else. Every meal, every song, every book will be unpalatable to someone.

5.5 Failure Is an Option

It's our survival instincts that help us judge when to take a risk of failure and when to retreat. But we've reprogrammed our instincts with the assumption that failure is not an option. So we stay home and protect ourselves from failure and deprive the world of our gifts.

It turns out that failure is not always something to be feared. We just have to reprogram our view of failure. When failure is a possibility, ask yourself these questions:

Is my goal worth the risk of failure? Many of us have an

CREATIVE GIANTS Bob Ross

BOB ROSS (1942–1995):
Bob Ross hosted the public television show *The Joy of Painting* from 1983 to 1994. During each half hour episode, Ross painted an elaborate landscape scene using techniques that any viewer at home could imitate. He seemed eternally at peace with his brush, painting "happy little trees." His calm demeanor endeared him to millions of people as his show was syndicated by public television stations across the country. Through his classes, hundreds of people have been certified to teach amateur painters Ross's techniques.

The man was not necessarily a fine artist. He openly admitted that his creations would never be in a museum. But Ross did a great thing for art. As an artist, he was a populist. He brought art to the people and told us that we could be artists without fear. His mission seemed to be to free adults from the bonds of self-consciousness and doubt. His greatest mantra, which he repeated over and over, was "We have no mistakes here, just happy accidents."

overblown sense of the consequences of failure. We imagine that we are still in junior high P.E. (or wherever your most embarrassing failures took place). The fact is, most of our failures are just not as consequential as we imagine they will be.

Are you measuring your goals and their risk accurately, or are you holding back your goals because you perceive failure to be too big a risk? Are your goals big enough that they are worth the risk of failure, or are you dreaming small goals just to avoid the possibility of failure?

Is success a real possibility? When you play a game, success is always a possibility. It is always possible to win, which makes the game fun, and even when you fail, you are able to learn from your mistakes. When you play against an opponent whose skill is so far beyond yours that victory is *not* possible, then playing is no longer fun.

As we grow up, we should have learned to discern which real life goals are attainable and which are not. The vast majority of little boys who dream of being baseball players realize after high school that this is not a realistic hope. But maybe the pendulum swung a little too hard for you, from childhood idealism to adult pessimism. How many adults never see their goals come to fruition, just because they give up too soon or do not work hard enough or imagine that failure is too great a risk?

Am I in control of my success or failure? Again, we can learn a bit about the real world from the fictional world of games. When I fail at a game or my opponent beats me, I still know that the game is fair. The game is not tricking me. There is no bug or flaw that makes success an impossibility. It is user error, every time.

It's only when success or failure is not in the hands of the player that the game is no longer worth playing. That's when we know the game is rigged.[6]

It is true that life is not fair. You will never accomplish every dream you ever dreamed because you were dealt a certain hand of cards at your birth. But too many adults become their own self-fulfilling prophecy of failure. We constantly blame our circumstances for our failings in life. We say that success was never really a possibility, or our failure is someone else's fault. We justify ourselves and say that life is just not fair, the game is rigged, and we protect our egos by not trying again.

So bad habits are not broken, or a marriage ends with "irreconcilable differences," or dreams are never realized.

But if you can answer yes to the three questions above, then the chances of success are high with just about any goal you have. The tools are available to you to achieve success. You just need the willpower to find them.

5.6 When Success Is Not Satisfying

There is one last thing about success and failure that we can learn from children.

Children understand (even if they cannot explain it) that success is cheapened and unsatisfying if it comes easily. A game in which everyone wins or a task in which success is not difficult is neither mentally engaging nor worth completing. An art project or a math assignment or a science experiment that does not stretch a student's abilities is boring and nothing to be proud of. Once again, low standards lose.

As an adult, I often find myself forgetting how truly resilient children can be in the face of failure. Children are often *eager* to try and fail, over and over again, to try to win a hard-fought victory and throw away their "participation" ribbons. It is the adult world that stomps on this childlike resiliency.

If you and I are going to stop living a "good enough" life, we're going to have to come to a few realizations:

Failure itself is not always such a terrible consequence. We may be embarrassed, but the world will not end.

Failure or success in life is usually in our own hands. Your circumstances in life are easy to blame for your failures, but they are often a scapegoat.

The most memorable people who shaped our lives never did so without their share of failure. Successful people don't learn how to avoid failing. They probably fail even more often than you or I, but that's only because they are trying to do more things.

The world needs you, and it needs your gifts. You must become generous with yourself again. But you will only become generous with yourself when you are able to release your fear of failure.

I struggle every day to suppress my fear of failure. That fear tells me I am just embarrassing myself and it would be better if I just stayed in bed. Fear wants to rob you and me of the joy of doing the things we were created to do.

What are we created to do? That is the final lesson of the art room.

QUESTIONS FOR THOUGHT

1. *What self-imposed limitations are you placing on your life because of your fear of failure? What are you not trying in order to avoid failure?*

2. *What would the consequences be if you failed? Embarrassment? Financial loss? Are the consequences really severe enough to keep you in fear? Is there a goal you can make for which the consequences of failure are not severe enough to deter you?*

3. *Are you happier and more content living inside your limitations, never knowing if you could succeed at something new?*

CHAPTER SIX

Born to *CREATE*

relearning how to be a creator

6.1 Meant to Create

I finished high school with a great senior art show, winning best overall portfolio. Ironically, I never joined the art club.

I had a lot of practice under my belt when I went to college to study graphic design. I was even invited to work for the department's private design studio. But something didn't feel right. I had my doubts about the career I was pursuing. And so the next few years, as with most twentysomethings, were a mix of struggles, victories, roadblocks, and breakthroughs. I pursued seminary, married my wife, moved into a tiny urban apartment, worked as a freelance designer (and it was just as dreadful as I imagined it).

I journeyed on, working as a pastor, and pursuing a career in education. I listened to well-wishers and felt the sting of rejection from one school after another. I realized I was being passed over by many principals because, although I was a passionate teacher, I could not also teach kids to throw a football or basketball. High schools and even middle schools need their male teachers to be coaches.

I quietly shook my fist at the heavens.

My lack of athleticism cursed me again. All that time I had spent learning math instead of shooting hoops—how foolish!

By my late twenties, I had been on artistic hiatus for five years. And still I had not found my real calling. I feared that I had wasted the best years of my life by pursuing a path that was closed to me. Creating had become unimportant to me. I had crashed into my personal limitations and was now terrified of continual failure, and I was willing to settle for just about anything and call it "good enough."

And then one day I received a very unexpected, providential phone call, for which I was completely unprepared.

The job I applied for had been filled. No surprise there.

But there was another opening to teach art.

It is true what Pablo Picasso said. The trick is to stay an artist as an adult. After years of study, struggle, frustration, exhaustion, and artistic exile, I was back to *creating* again. My art room has become one of the greatest, most challenging, and most satisfying creations of my life.

6.2 The Last Day of School

Today is the last day of art class with my sixth graders.

They are officially full-fledged junior high students after this one last hour, the last remnant of their elementary education. After this, the math and science will continue to get more complex. Their interests and priorities will continue to evolve.

Already they are so much different than they were when they first stepped into the art room on their first day of kindergarten. They have become so self-conscious. They are aware that every move they make, every victory and defeat they have, will be measured and judged by their peers. They are beginning to learn to live within their limitations. They have decided that some things are worth trying and many things are not. They are becoming hardened in their aversion to failure. Failure looks bad to others. It causes embarrassment. Staying inside one's limitations should minimize failure and the accompanying humiliation. They can deflect attention from their feelings of inadequacy in much the same way I did in P.E. They can pretend they are not trying by purposefully messing up their work and blowing off class.

For many of them, *creating* has long lost its importance. Soon they will stop making cards for Mother's Day and simply use their money to buy a card. They will stop having original questions and will be tempted to start plagiarizing the ideas of others. They are forming habits that will follow them for a lifetime. For many of them, life will revolve around the pursuit of gaining as much as possible with as little effort as possible. Laziness will be its own reward. Low standards will be a cardinal virtue. For most of them, this will be the last time they ever set foot inside an art room again, at least until they bring their own children to their first day of school.

It is a poignant moment. In a few minutes, they will no longer be mine.

I hope that the art room has meant something to them, besides "craft time" or an extra recess. Something profound or spiritual. Because already these kids are getting a taste of the ugliness of the world. But I'd like to warn them that there's more ugliness in store for them—*a lot more.*

I remember the first time one of my friend's parents got divorced. It was ugly. And some years later, my friend's mother died of a very ugly sickness. Later, it was so strange when I found myself at the stage in life when *my own* friends and acquaintances began divorcing. Families breaking apart is ugly.

Others among my peers became addicted. Some of the girls became addicted to the attention of boys who were no good for them. Some of the guys drank way more than was good for them. While I was working as a grocery cashier, an old man would come through my checkout line. He was usually disheveled and his breath smelled like vodka, and the only thing he wanted from the store was another fifth of liquor. And I thought to myself, *Some people my age, someone I know, will become like this man.* Addiction is ugly.

What a strange feeling picking up my purple dorm room phone in December of my freshman year. It was my mother calling to tell me my friend was dead. He was sailing a small catamaran with two friends on a notoriously windy lake in Kansas. Death, when it is untimely, is ugly.

And as we grew up, childhood friends grew apart, became estranged, or violently broke company as we all tried to cope with the ugly adult world we were now a part of.

Of course, only the ugliest aspects of humanity make the news. It still amazes me to see how ugly people can be toward one another on such a large scale. It is as if humanity itself is addicted to ugliness. We hate it, but we cannot stop making it. There's a proverb in the Bible that talks about how a dog will throw up, walk away, and then come back and eat its own vomit.

The proverb says that is what humanity is like.

The writer calls it like he sees it. People are like dogs eating their own barf. We keep drinking from the same poisoned well. We keep going back to the same ugliness. We keep eating what we already rejected. We settle for "good enough," and so often, "good enough" is nowhere close to "good." It is ugly.

6.3 An Unfinished Life

One summer, I took a short-term mission trip to Mexico. I traveled alone and met a group of other Americans from all over the country who had signed on for the same trip.

Our missionary hosts met us at the airport and we crammed into vans that lacked air-conditioning. The drive to our destination was long. We traveled along dusty roads through vast, scrubby-looking okra fields, dotted with workers carrying huge baskets on their backs.

Eventually the fields disappeared and we entered the town we would temporarily call home. Our guide explained the three types of houses that exist in these kinds of rural Mexican communities. About half the houses we saw were nothing more than shanties, built by hand with scraps of tin and plywood. Some shanties were equipped with small creature comforts, like a window air conditioner or a water tank on the roof. Skinny horses drank water from the irrigation ditches along the road while roosters ran around yards, pestering hens.

The second kind of house, almost making up the other half of the community, belonged to the "middle-class" families. These homes were made of concrete. The thick walls, I assume, kept the inside somewhat cool. They were short, single story, bunker-like cubes.

Of course, when you build a concrete structure, you place steel rebar rods in the concrete to reinforce the structure. The curious thing about the concrete homes was that almost all of them had the rebar rods sticking *out* of the tops of the walls, like dozens of antennae. To any American, the houses looked sloppy and the construction looked unfinished and unprofessional. Who leaves rebar sticking out of the top of their house?

The steel rods were there for a reason though.

The third type of house—and there were very few of them— was a concrete house with a second floor. Someone in this community had really done well if he could afford to build a house with a second floor.

That was why all the rebar was sticking out of the single story houses. The rebar represented *unmet ambitions.* They were unfinished business; dreams that had not been achieved yet. The rebar was left exposed *in the hope* that the family could one day add a second floor onto their house. When they were able to achieve that, they would know they had succeeded in life.

Chances are good that you are very much like one of my sixth graders. You have not set foot in an art room in years. And you have seen a lot of ugliness in the time since.

And since then, a lot of things have happened in your own life. You have pursued education or a career or maybe military service. Maybe you got married and started a family. Perhaps you bought a house and now have lots of bills to be concerned with. You work hard to support your family. You have a few friends you see on the Fourth of July or at the Christmas party.

Maybe your life has turned out the way you wanted. But chances are good that not all of it has been what you expected or wanted. Your life has been a process of your childhood optimism crashing into a world that does not seem to care, your ambitions and passions being chipped away by other, more toilsome concerns. Maybe your work feels unimportant and your life feels somewhat meaningless. Maybe you are still trying to erase big mistakes you made when you were less wise. Maybe you are embittered about your lot in life and blame others for how your life has played out.

In other words, maybe it feels like you still have a bunch of steel rods sticking out of your house. Your life feels *incomplete*. You are faced with the feeling that you aren't meeting your potential, that your ambitions and dreams will have to remain *unfinished*, and that reality leaves you with an undeniable, unshakeable anxiety about your life and purpose.

6.4 You Are a Creator

Here's the last art room lesson. This is what it is all about. It is time to peel back that final layer of crusty old paint that has hardened around you over the years. This is the lesson you should've learned on that last day of art class before being sent out into junior high school, and the rest of your life:

You *are* a creator.

Yes, you are. Maybe you are not an *artist.* Maybe since you left the art room, you have never picked up a paintbrush or a piece of chalk since. But you are a creator. I know you are a creator, because you are made in the image of a Creator. You carry the Creator's image and creative spark. You were *created* to create.

Maybe you don't feel "creative" at all! Maybe it has been so long since you thought about creating that you cannot wrap your mind around this. Maybe you say you have far more pressing, adult concerns and you don't have time or energy to think about creating.

It is true I am suggesting what may be a *massive* shift in how you view yourself. I am suggesting that you can look at your entire life and purpose through the prism of creating. This may not be easy for you to accept.

But consider this: perhaps the anxiety that you feel about your life, your purpose, and all of your hopes and ambitions is due to the fact that you have been looking at them all wrong. What if seeing yourself in focus, for the first time, as you really are solved all the mystery you feel about your life?

6.5 **Everyday Creator**

As you learn to embrace what you are about to read, you will more easily begin to embrace the suggestion that you are a born creator.

Here's what I want you to understand first:

You cannot help creating.

You have never *stopped* creating.

You just stopped *thinking* about creating.

When you were a child, you did not think about creating, you just did it. You were at your best when you were creating something to share with the people you loved. And even though that creative spark has been stifled and hidden and snuffed out by other cares, you have still been creating. You have been creating every day, just without thinking about it. Every day, you add a few more brushstrokes to your life.

Or maybe, you've been using your eraser a bit too much. Your life looks rather unfinished and incomplete. Maybe there are large patches of your life that used to be full of color, but you've rubbed it away. Or you have been careless and have let things get kind of messy and life isn't turning out the way you envisioned it in your head.

The second point to understand about being a creator is this: Humans are born naturally creative, and we remain this way *because it is how we are created*.

We were created to rule and subdue the earth, to reshape it as we see fit. When humans see a problem or experience some kind of discomfort or frustration, we create a solution.

When you embrace the reality that you are a creator, you are *finally* embracing *how you were made*. You are embracing the identity that God created for you. When you embrace your job or your politics or your sexuality as *the* key feature of your identity, you are embracing only a small, partial identity, rather than the broad, sweeping, *full* identity that God created you to fulfill.

The third point to understand is this: the more you embrace the lessons of chapters 3, 4, and 5, the more your heart and mind will be prepared to embrace this final lesson.

In chapter 3, we discussed the problem of living "good enough." You cannot embrace life as a creator if you are content to settle for "good enough." Good enough is your status quo. Good enough is the low standards you've been taught to set for yourself and is the source of your anxiety.

In chapter 4, we talked about being defeated by our limitations. You cannot be a creator if you will not come to terms with your limitations.

Chapter 5 was all about fear of failure. You cannot be a creator if you are afraid of failing.

Master those fears, and you are on your way to mastering life as a creator.

Fourth, remember this: creations always say something about their creator.

Look around at what you've created with your life. Take an inventory. What does it all say about you? Have you been mindful of what you've been creating? Has it been purposeful? Art that is created without a lot of attention doesn't usually turn out well. Neither does a life that doesn't have a lot of attention given to it. You will be creating for the rest of your life. You might as well do it on purpose.

CREATIVE GIANTS Family

No one more profoundly creates our childhood than our parents. What kind of creators were your parents?

Mine aren't especially creative people in the artistic sense. But they created plenty in their own rights. My parents did not create a perfect childhood. Who does? We are constrained by imperfection. But within the imperfection, they created a lot of beauty.

They created a home where love and learning and spirituality was important, where everyone was celebrated. Mom stayed home with us as toddlers and created a lifelong love of learning. Dad impressed on my brother and me that we were inheriting a family name that was not wealthy or powerful but had taken decades for my grandparents to create.

My maternal grandfather was the precise engineer, but my paternal grandfather was the type who was comfortable with "jerry-rigging" things. When we went fishing, his tackle box was full of miscellaneous lures. His Christmas lights were all mismatched. When one burned out, it was replaced with whatever was close at hand.

But Grandma and Grandpa were meticulous about other matters. They made their living by running grocery stores. Not a very creative profession, you might think. These were small town stores in the 1950s and 60s with just a few employees each. Grandma kept the books while Grandpa managed the business. Since they lived for a few years in California, they had developed a taste for citrus and Mexican foods that were unknown in rural Missouri. Their stores were the only ones in town to stock lemon flavored candies and tortillas. They probably took home more of those products than they sold.

When they bought their first store, it had a reputation among the town's poorest residents for selling the cheapest ground meat in town, at just nine cents a pound. On the last day of the outgoing owner's tenure, he showed Grandpa the magical secret of nine-cent meat. In the back room was the meat grinder and a huge vat of prepared meat ready to be packaged. The shopkeeper added a very liberal helping of stale cracker crumbs and water. His secret of affordability wasn't magic. It was filler. It was "good enough" for poor people.

When Grandpa opened the store the next day, the price of meat had tripled, much to the righteous indignation of the housewives. But it also featured a money-back guarantee. The shoppers grudgingly took their meat home, feeling ripped off, and later prepared dinner. It was not until that evening that those poor people learned that water

was not supposed to come out of the meat when it hit the skillet. They realized they had been buying junk for years. No one returned their purchases.

Even when serving poor, often illiterate, small town people, they created a reputation of being "good," not "good enough." They treated people with respect and gave away endless amounts of groceries. The inheritance their children would one day receive was given away a bag of food at a time. Even the stuff they gave away did not have useless junk filler in it.

My family worked endlessly to create good things for us. I cannot repay it. All I can do is turn around and create good things for others.

6.6 Beauty or Ugliness

I have made a big deal about being a creator, and now you're wondering *what it is you are supposed to be creating.*

That is a great question.

What we are meant to create is the same for you and me and every sixth grader who leaves my room. When you set your mind on this, you will master your identity as a creator, and your life will be changed.

Here it is: beauty.

The world is full of ugliness. It is desperately searching for beauty. And even the beauty that the world thinks it finds is usually ugliness in disguise. People live in ugliness, they create ugliness, they eat ugliness, they dream about ugliness, they bathe in ugliness, they worship ugliness, they die in ugliness. We have learned to settle for this and accept ugliness and even to call ugliness "beauty," because we do not know any different. Ugliness is cheap, disposable, formulaic; and it saturates us, while beauty is exceedingly rare.

You are affected by ugliness every day. It cannot be helped. But what are you going to leave behind? What is going to be the product of your life?

What are you going to create today: *beauty* or *ugliness*?

That is it.

Is the product, the sum total, the legacy of your life *beautiful* or *ugly*?

This is the "good" life: a life that creates beauty, that doesn't settle for the cheap, the ugly, the disposable. It doesn't have to be complicated. Beauty can be very simple. Jesus said that when someone offers a cup of water to someone in His name, we are really offering a cup of water to Him. I imagine that what Jesus says is true of a cup of water is true of a cupcake too. Cups of water and cupcakes are pretty simple. Most acts of beauty are like that.

Beauty is not about making your life look like a Pinterest board so all your friends can see how crafty you are. Beauty is a choice you make, a profound, life-changing choice.

Jesus confronted people every day who were mired in ugliness. While sitting at a well, He got a woman to open up to Him, who had been married five times and was currently living with a man who wasn't her husband. While walking through a town, He lunched with Zaccheus, a tax man who had spent his life robbing his countrymen. And everywhere He went, Jesus confronted Pharisees who habitually created ugliness in the name of the Creator of all beauty. (Some things, unfortunately, never change.)

Everywhere Jesus went, He asked people to give up creating and living in worthless, ugly things. He told them they needed to embrace a new identity. He told them they must be more like the children.

So what kind of a child were you? Were you climbing trees and playing in the mud? Then go get your hands dirty. Were you making up stories? Then make up a great story and *live it.* Were you building with blocks? Then find a complex problem and create an elegant solution.

Just because you are a *former* kindergartner, it doesn't mean your life is over.

You can make time every day to joyfully, generously, unabashedly create beauty. Every day is a new canvas to paint on. Every interaction you have with the world is a chance to add a little more paint—at work or at home or while being served your coffee or wherever else you find yourself today.

Your quest to create beauty might be grand in scale. You might have high ambitions. You may travel to faraway places and help erase ugliness globally. Or you may specialize in tiny bursts of beauty that have a powerful impact. You may be able to turn your quest for beauty into a revenue stream, so you can quit your job, if that is your desire. Or maybe you'll have to keep your job to support your ambitions. Maybe you actually have the skills to reach your goals; or perhaps, like a movie producer, you have a great vision and you are able to mobilize other people to help reach your goals.

You never know how far the beauty you create will reach. It reaches far beyond ourselves, out into the world. Who taught Michelangelo to sculpt? Who taught Martin Luther how to read his Bible? Who taught Mozart how to compose music? They are people who don't make the history books, but they created *other people*. Without those anonymous creators, there is no history.

Whatever beauty exists in your life, go be fruitful and multiply it. Fill the earth with it. Even a small, beautiful thing has the power to change bigger things. Once people get a taste of genuine, authentic beauty, they want more. They realize the inferiority and the ugliness of everything else.

A little bit of beauty can change *everything*.

6.7 Beauty Is Fragile

Beauty, in this world, is extremely fragile.

When Leonardo da Vinci was preparing to paint his masterpiece, *The Last Supper*, he wanted to create a new technique in painting. Artists of the day typically painted in fresco, which meant applying pigment to wet plaster. With such a technique, a skilled artist could render a face in about the space of a day.

Da Vinci did not want to work in this manner for this project.

He wanted to be able to move around the painting, to work all around, rather than focusing on one spot and then not touching it again once it was dry.

The Last Supper was an immediate and stunning success. It defines da Vinci's genius with layers of subtle symbolism and perspective. The problem was that da Vinci's new painting technique was *not* a success. Fresco paintings are delicate, but his experiment was an absolute failure. The painting was badly decayed even by the time its creator died. It has remained a challenge for art conservers ever since.

Incredible amounts of time and money are spent attempting to restore and preserve priceless works of art because they are so fragile. Next time you go to a museum, you may notice little boxes that look like bombs sitting in each room. Those devices are measuring every possible atmospheric variable that could damage the paintings. The greatest fear of art museums is perhaps not that a piece of work will be stolen but that a stolen work will be returned irreparably damaged.

Paintings are not the only fragile beauty. The whole catalog of humanity's achievements is threatened with destruction every day. The earth exists to erode, to rust, to destroy man's work. Throw mankind's own foolishness into the mix, with our wars and dark ages, and you realize one of the greatest tragedies is all the beauty that has been lost to the ages.

Paintings are just like the beauty in your life today. They are extraordinarily fragile.

The beauty of a marriage is extraordinarily fragile, relying on the tensile strands of trust between two fallible, imperfect, sometimes foolish people. Relationships with our children are extremely complicated and fragile endeavors. Our health—physical, mental, and spiritual—rests precariously on a precipice.

It takes a lot less effort to destroy something beautiful than it takes to create it. A beautiful marriage is more easily destroyed than built. Trust is more easily broken than gained. Societal harmony is easier broken then mended. It is much easier to slowly let go of one's health than to maintain it. It is easier to be indifferent in the face of injustice. It is easier to stay silent when a lonely young man is denied a seat with his peers in a restaurant. It is easier to destroy our relationships, careers, reputations, bodies, minds, and spiritual conditions than it is to build them into beautiful things.

It was exceedingly easier for mankind to fall than it was for God to redeem His beloved and fragile creation from sin.

When resolving to create beauty in the world, remember this: beauty is fragile. It is precious. It takes a lot more work to create beauty than it does to destroy it. Creating beauty will be meaningful but difficult work. This is not the place for laziness or fearfulness. And all along the way, ugliness will be crouching at your door, waiting to steal it from you.

6.8 What Will Beauty Look Like?

This I know: when you embrace your role as a creator in this world, your life can change. You can have a new perspective on your aspirations, ambitions, and purpose.

And when you embrace your role as a creator of *beauty*, the world can be changed.

But there is the sticking point. I cannot give you a formula for beauty. No one can. We can describe beauty or point out beauty, but no one can turn beauty into a formula.

Only you can make the conscious decision to use your life to create beauty. And only you can decide *how* you will create it. There is no paint-by-numbers that will erase all the ugliness from your life. There's always an element of the unknown when people create. We don't *quite* know how the finished product will turn out. We will probably make some mistakes along the way, or maybe some happy accidents. Maybe we will even surprise ourselves.

I cannot tell you exactly what beauty is going to look like in your life. But like most of the wonderful, mysterious, joyful things in this world that you cannot quite explain, you will know it when you see it.

QUESTIONS FOR THOUGHT

1. *What is my life creating: beauty or ugliness?*
2. *Who is affected by the beauty of ugliness I create? Who am I creating for?*

NOTES

1. Andres Duany, Elizabeth Plater-Zyberk, Jeff Speck. *Suburban Nation: The Rise of Sprawl and the Decline of the American Dream*. New York: North Point Press, 2010.

2. Amy Hollingsworth. *The Simple Faith of Mister Rogers: Spiritual Insights on the World's Most Beloved Neighbor*. Brentwood, TN: Integrity Publishers, 2005.

3. Joseph T. Hallinan. *Why We Make Mistakes: How We Look without Seeing, Forget Things in Seconds, and Are All Pretty Sure We Are Way Above Average*. New York: Random House, 2009.

4. Donald Pease. *Theodore Seuss Geisel*. New York: Oxford University Press, 2010.

5. Nick Paumgarten. "Master of Play." *The New Yorker*. December 20, 2010. http://www.newyorker.com/reporting/2010/12/20/101220fa_fact_paumgarten.

6. Jane McGonigal. *Reality Is Broken: Why Games Make Us Better and How They Can Change the World*. New York: Penguin Press, 2011.

ACKNOWLEDGMENTS

First of all, let me sincerely thank you, the reader of this book. Please take this moment to write your name in the blank space below, so that you will be duly acknowledged:

Matt Appling would like to thank _____ _____ for reading this book. I hope I get to meet you and give you a proper thanks.

If I were to acknowledge everyone to whom I owe a debt in writing this book, I believe I would have to write an entirely separate book filled with names, and no one would read that.

In lieu of that option, please know that even if I am not able to mention you by name, you have been in my mind throughout my time with this book.

This book would simply not exist without the thoughtful

encouragement of Darrell and Ally Vesterfelt. Thank you for being my cheerleaders and advocates on this project before it was even an idea. Thank you to the team at Moody Publishers for taking a chance on me and for all your dedication in making my work so much better.

I owe a debt of thanks to so many people who have either loved me, believed in me, put up with me, or some combination of all three throughout many years, for without your contribution in creating me, this book would not exist: my family, friends, and church, most especially Cheri, Mom and Dad, Aaron and Tanya, Miles and June, Wally and Dot, Don and Susie, Andrew, Tim, Christy, Jake, Nickie, Jason, Rena, Joel, Rachel, Heath, Amber, John, Kip, Trina, Ainsley, Susan, Darlene, Carson, Les, Wayne, Patty, Brandon, and many others.

I must acknowledge all of my students who inspire and challenge me every day, though they will almost certainly never read this book.

I am stunned to think of all of the people who have let me pretend to be a writer, people who have read what I have written, given comments, cheers, or criticisms, even while your own writing has often moved and convicted me. Special thanks in this regard goes to Kathy Richards, Helen Mignon, David Johndrow, Joel Bezaire, Billy Coffey, Jason Elkins, John Cowart, Peter Pollock, K. C. Proctor, Sonny Lemmons, Nicole Cottrell, Rachel Held Evans, Matthew Paul Turner, Kyle Reed, Alece Ronzino, Anne Jackson, Jamie Wright, Lindsey Nobles, Tamara Lunardo, Justin Davis, Tony C., Brian Russell, Jay Adams, Ken Hagerman, Jeremy Statton, Zack Hunt, Wes Molebash, Jeff Goins,

Ed Cyzewski, Duane Scott, Tony Alicia, Tor Constantino, Seth Caddell, Paul Angone et al. There are dozens and dozens of you, and you know who you are.

Of course, if you find yourself somewhere in this book, in name, or in thought, thank you for being so much more interesting than me.

And of course, my art teachers: thank you for helping to keep this child artist alive.

HOW DO YOU PACK FOR ALL FIFTY STATES?

978-0-8024-0729-0

When I was in college, I figured my life would come together around graduation. I'd meet a guy; we'd plan a beautiful wedding and buy a nice house—not necessarily with a picket fence, but with whatever kind of fence we wanted. I might work, or I might not, but whatever we decided, I would be happy.

When I got out of college and my life didn't look like that, I floundered, trying to figure out how to get the life I had always dreamed of. Just when I had given up all hope of finding the "life I'd always dreamed about," I decided to take a trip to all fifty states . . . because when you go on a trip, you can't take your baggage. What I found was that "packing light" wasn't as easy as I thought it was.

This is the story of that trip and learning to live life with less baggage.

MOODY
PUBLISHERS
www.MoodyPublishers.com

moody
collective

Moody Collective brings words of life to a generation seeking deeper faith. We are a part of Moody Publishers, representing this next generation of followers of Christ through books, blogs, essays, and more.

We seek to know, love, and serve the millennial generation with grace and humility. Each of our books is intended to challenge and encourage our readers as they pursue God. To learn more, visit our website, www.moodycollective.com.

www.MoodyPublishers.com